ScriptureWalk Senior High Youth Themes

ScriptureWalk Senior High
Youth Themes

Bible-Based Sessions for Teens

Michael Theisen
Nora Bradbury-Haehl

Saint Mary's Press
Christian Brothers Publications
Winona, Minnesota

Genuine recycled paper with 10% post-consumer waste.
Printed with soy-based ink.

From Nora:

Thank you Barry, Amy, Tom, Patrick, Therese, Eric, Kathy, Jan, Ursula, Lee, and Monica for all the learning and laughing together.

A special thank you to the teenagers at Saint Joseph's Parish, Penfield, New York, and Holy Trinity Parish, Webster, New York, especially the youth leaders and GROOP staff, for their insight.

Thank you to Michael Theisen for walking with me through this and for his encouragement, and to the Bradbury family.

From Michael and Nora:

We are indebted to the writing and publishing team of *The Catholic Youth Bible* for their commitment to and understanding of young people, which has made all of this possible. Thank you for your great effort.

The publishing team included Brian Singer-Towns, development editor; Mary Duerson, copy editor; Barbara Bartelson, production editor; Hollace Storkel, typesetter; Stephan Nagel, art director; Alicia María Sánchez, cover designer; pre-press, printing, and binding by the graphics division of Saint Mary's Press.

*"And the Word became flesh and lived among us" (John 1:14a).
To Mary, Christopher, David, and Rachel for incarnating the Word in
our home and in my heart.*

Michael (Dad)

*To Monica, Gregory, and Catherine for hugs and knock-knock jokes and
testing out the good Samaritan story. To Greg for love and patience.*

Nora

Contents

Introduction

The Reason for the ScriptureWalk Series

The search for both meaning and mystery is a powerful quest with young people, especially as they begin to form their own personal worldview during adolescence. As young people journey through this stage of life, they begin to ask important spiritual questions, such as How did life start?, Why do bad things happen to good or innocent people?, What is my purpose?, Where is God?, and even, Is God?

In the search for answers to these questions, the Bible shines like a beacon. Within the Bible's pages, God's word sheds light on both the meaning and the mystery of life. The more young people are assisted in reading and reflecting on the powerful messages contained in the Scriptures, the better equipped they will be for the spiritual journey, both individually and communally.

Vatican Council II opened the doors for Catholics to read and study the Bible with renewed fervor. In the last few decades, parish Scripture study groups have sprung up across the country as Catholic adults began to enthusiastically explore the Bible. However, the Catholic scriptural renewal has yet to fully flower among Catholic young people, partly owing to a lack of resources designed to engage Catholic young people in Bible study and reflection. The ScriptureWalk series is designed to help fill that gap.

Bringing the Scripture to Life

God speaks to us through the Bible whomever we are and wherever we are and whatever age we might be. The Bible is a source of strength and a source of challenge. The Scriptures have an incredible power to transform our life. If we invite the Scriptures off the written page and into our life and heart, we cannot help but be changed in a radical way. The *ScriptureWalk Senior High* sessions in this book will help you in making the Bible come alive for your senior high youth.

The Goals of *ScriptureWalk Senior High: Youth Themes*

ScriptureWalk Senior High: Youth Themes has four goals:
* That the young people study the Bible using a group process that is consistent with Catholic scriptural interpretation

- That the young people apply the Bible's teachings to important issues in their life
- That volunteer youth or adult leaders use the session components in a variety of settings
- That the young people are motivated to read and reflect on the Scriptures as a part of their regular prayer life

In addressing these goals, this volume of the ScriptureWalk series contains eight sessions on themes that concern senior high youth today. The themes were chosen based on a survey of Catholic youth that asked which topics they would most like to explore in the Bible. The Bible passages used with each theme were carefully selected to speak authentically to the topic.

The Structure of *ScriptureWalk Senior High*

All the *ScriptureWalk Senior High* books give group leaders a great deal of flexibility in how they use the session components. Each session is divided into three separate but interrelated components. These components can be used together to create a 90-minute session on a particular theme, they can be used separately to enhance other events, or they can be combined in various ways to create new activities. To facilitate this independent use, each of the three components starts on a new page and has its own list of needed materials. When appropriate, special instructions are included for using a component as an independent activity. Each component is also designated by a special icon. The icon appears at the top of every page containing directions for that component. This will help in quickly locating the directions for a specific component. The icons with descriptions of the three components follow:

 **Study It**

The first component of every session in this book is called Study It and takes 45 to 60 minutes. The Study It component is essentially a five-step Bible study process on the session theme. The steps are described more fully in this introduction, in the section titled "Leading the Study It Component."

 Live It

The second component of each session is called Live It. It consists of a 15- to 30-minute activity engaging the young people in the session topic in an active and thought-provoking way. The Live It component can lead them to better understand how the Bible's teaching on the topic can be lived out today.

In addition to the primary activity, we have included an alternative approach for the Live It component. It gives you an option to consider using with your group. Like the primary activity, it engages the young people in a fun and active way, but it is described in less detail. After you have looked over the primary activity, consider the potential of the alternative approach for fitting your group's interest.

Pray It

The third component of each session is Pray It, a 10- to 15-minute prayer service on the theme of the session's Scripture passage. The prayer services use guided meditation, shared prayer, music, silence, and reflective readings. The Pray It component gives the young people an opportunity to bring their insights and concerns to God in prayer.

Suggestions for Program Leaders

Where and When Should I Use These Sessions?

The active-learning techniques and small-group discussions of *ScriptureWalk Senior High* sessions make them ideal for use with either high school youth groups or catechetical programs. The sessions are arranged alphabetically by topic. They do not build on one another, so you can use them independently whenever your group wants (or needs!) to study a particular topic. Or you can use all eight sessions as a semester course on life issues. You can create 60- to 90-minute (or even longer) sessions by using one, two, or three of the components.

Keep in mind that each of the three session components can stand on its own and be used independently. This allows for great flexibility in how you use them. For example, a group of young people meeting after school for an hour-long Bible study might use only the Study It and Pray It portions of a session. Or a parish youth ministry coordinator might choose to use all three components of a session as one integrated activity during a retreat. In still another setting, a young leader might decide to use the Pray It component from the friendship session to conclude a youth group meeting on friendship.

Consider how you might use the *ScriptureWalk Senior High* components in the following settings:
- Catholic high school religion classes
- youth group meetings
- retreats
- parish religious education classes
- Confirmation preparation classes
- leadership training sessions
- mentor programs
- intergenerational activities

What Group Size Works with These Sessions?

The time estimates for the session components are based on a group size of ten to fifteen young people. However, by slightly adjusting the session plans, they can be used with groups as small as five or as large as sixty. For example, when doing a discussion exercise with a large group, invite only a limited number of participants to share their thoughts. Or break the large group into smaller groups. Look over the session plan in advance to determine which activities will work better with a large group and which will work better with small groups.

For discussions in the Study It components, it is important to work in groups of five to eight young people, thus allowing everyone more opportunity to share their thoughts on the Bible passage and the discussion questions. If you are doing several topics from *Scripture-Walk Senior High* with the same large group, you may want to keep the small discussion groups consistent from session to session to encourage deeper sharing over time.

What Bible Should I Use?

Ideally, every person participating in *ScriptureWalk Senior High* will have his or her own Bible to use. This can help the participants become more comfortable in using the Bible. Use a Catholic edition containing both the Old and New Testaments. Avoid translations that use archaic language (like the King James version) or paraphrasing (like the Living Bible). The New American Bible and the Catholic edition of the New Revised Standard Version are good choices.

We strongly recommend using a youth-friendly study Bible such as *The Catholic Youth Bible,* published by Saint Mary's Press. Such Bibles commonly contain helpful background articles and introductions to individual books of the Bible that can enrich the participants' knowledge and discussion.

Leading the Study It Component

The Study It component is the heart of each *ScriptureWalk Senior High* session. It has a consistent five-step format. The steps are explained below with suggestions for leading each one.

Step 1: Opening activity
Each session starts with a catchy, short activity introducing the participants to the session theme. The activities are simple and take 10 minutes or less. If your group is large, the opening activity could be done as a large group. Or you could break the group into small groups of five to eight before the opening activity and have the young people stay in their group for the whole Bible study. You can designate a young person in each group as its facilitator. Or you may wish to have young adult or adult facilitators.

Step 2: Proclamation
In this step the Scripture passage chosen to address the session topic is proclaimed. Proclaiming the Scriptures is different from simply reading them. Proclamation implies an intentional reading, done with feeling and conviction. You may proclaim the reading yourself, or you may ask a participant to do it. If you have a large group that has already divided into small groups, assign and prepare a reader for each group. Give the person or persons proclaiming the passage some time to practice. Be sure the person proclaiming the passage in each group does not disturb the other groups by reading too loudly.

Have group members follow along in their Bible while the passage is being read. Although reading along in this way would not be appropriate in a eucharistic liturgy, it is appropriate and even desirable for a Bible study.

Step 3: Initial reaction

In this step the young people briefly react to the Scripture passage they have just heard. Believers are convinced that God does speak to us through the Bible. An age-old practice for helping us listen to what God is saying is to listen for words, phrases, or stories that strike a chord within us. Three or four reflection questions in this step help the young people do that. Emphasize that the questions have no right or wrong answers. And do not try to force the discussion of them to go on too long. Usually, 5 to 10 minutes suffice.

If your group is large and you have not already divided it into small groups, do so for this step. Each discussion group may have five to eight people. The young people will work in these small groups for this discussion and the final discussion in step 5.

Step 4: Commentary

After the initial reaction to the Scripture passage, the leader presents a brief commentary on the passage. The commentary gives background on the passage's historical situation and the church's interpretation of it. This sets the stage for the application step, in which the young people apply the passage to their life today. The commentary helps them make this application in light of the church's understanding of the passage, rather than entirely based on their personal interpretation.

You can deliver the commentary in several ways:

- Read it out loud to the group as it is written.
- Photocopy it and give a copy to each participant to read over silently, or ask one person to read it out loud while the others follow along.
- Present it in your own words. Write the major points out on newsprint to add emphasis.
- If you have formed small discussion groups, designate a reader in each group and give her or him a copy of it to read aloud.

Regardless of the method employed, this step should be short and simple, no more than 5 minutes.

Step 5: Application

The final step is a sharing exercise in which the group's initial reaction and the commentary are connected to the experience of young people today. Depending on how comfortable the participants are with one another, and on how talkative they tend to be, this step can last 15 to 30 minutes. Allow enough time for the young people to really grapple with the implications of the biblical message.

Given your knowledge of the young people in your group, before the session, review the discussion questions in this step and decide which ones to ask and which ones to drop. Rephrase or add questions if you think doing so might spark discussion better.

Challenge each participant to search for her or his personal answers to the reflection questions. Do not allow a few participants to dominate the discussion. One good strategy for involving everyone is to first ask the participants to journal or reflect quietly on a question or set of questions for a couple of minutes. Then invite them to share their reflections out loud. This allows the more introverted members time to formulate their responses and encourages the extroverted members to think more deeply about their answers.

Prepare, Prepare, Prepare!

Prepare for a session by reading over its components and deciding which ones to use. Become familiar with the commentary in the Study It component. If necessary, look up additional background in a Bible commentary or a Bible dictionary (see the resources at the end of this introduction). Be sure to gather the necessary supplies and take care of any other preparations. To help you with this, each component begins with a materials needed list and, when appropriate, a list of other necessary preparations. Be sure to look for these lists for each component that you are using.

Put Together a Supply Box

Many of the same materials are needed for each session. You can save time by collecting these materials in a supply box and having it on hand for each session. We recommend that the box include the following items:
- Bibles, one for each person
- pens or pencils
- markers
- scrap paper
- newsprint
- several pairs of scissors
- a candle and matches
- a tape or CD player, and recordings of reflective instrumental music
- masking tape
- a Bible concordance
- a Bible commentary

Involve the Participants

When conducting *ScriptureWalk Senior High* sessions or activities, use young people in leadership roles as much as possible. One of the best ways to learn about something is to teach it to others. So as you prepare for a session, consider ways in which participants can be invited to lead parts of each component. You might ask them to proclaim a reading, lead a prayer experience, or conduct a group discussion. Any of the session readings or directions can be photocopied for this purpose. When group members are involved, they are more likely to learn and grow.

Adapt the Components to Fit Your Group

Like individuals, each group is unique. To use a session exactly as it is written may not be the most effective strategy for your group. While preparing for the session, think of the unique traits of your group members. Which session questions, activities, or prayers seem to speak to them and their life situations? Which do not? Can the latter be altered or adjusted to make them relevant? Often, slightly changing the wording of a question or adding a step to an activity can make the difference between a successful group experience and an incredibly successful group experience!

Set Up an Appealing Environment

Even the most prepared group leader will have a difficult time getting the group members involved if the meeting environment is uncomfortable, uninviting, or distracting. Take time to evaluate your physical environment:

- Provide sufficient light. The room should be neither too bright nor too dark.
- Avoid areas with continual distractions: doors being opened and closed, phones ringing, or people walking by.
- Consider having snacks and beverages available for participants before the session or during a break.
- Arrange the chairs for small groups in a circle to reflect the idea that everyone in the group is on equal ground.

Also notice the relational environment. Make the participants feel welcome. Actions like the following can make a big difference:

- Warmly greet the participants by name.
- Help group members learn and use one another's names throughout the session.
- As new people enter the group, invite the current members to welcome and orient them.

Session Follow-up Ideas

ScriptureWalk Senior High provides two tools to help the young people continue their reflection after the session, either individually or with their family. The first tool is a short section at the end of each session called Family Connection. This section gives a simple, family-based follow-up idea for the session. You may wish to send the ideas home in a newsletter, photocopy them for the participants, or simply suggest them to the young people at the end of the session.

The second tool is a bookmark containing five Scripture passages and related questions for individuals to use for reflection or journaling after each session. A different bookmark has been created specifically for each session. They are grouped together in appendix B of this manual. Photocopy the bookmarks for your group. Note that many of the Scripture passages on the bookmarks are also connected to informative articles in *The Catholic Youth Bible,* published by Saint Mary's Press.

Interpreting the Scriptures

Contextualism Versus Fundamentalism

ScriptureWalk Senior High uses a contextualist approach to interpreting the Scriptures. Contextualism is one of two very different approaches that Christians take in interpreting the Scriptures. The other approach, often referred to as fundamentalism, views all the stories and information in the Bible as historical and scientific fact. For example, a fundamentalist approach insists that God did in fact create the world in six 24-hour days.

Like the fundamentalist approach, the contextualist approach believes the Bible is true and without error in teaching the things God wants us to know for our salvation. But the contextualist approach does not insist that all the stories and information in the Bible must be interpreted as historical and scientific fact. A contextualist approach keeps in mind the literary genre or style of a particular book, the cultural background of the inspired author's original audience, and the church's ongoing teaching about the particular passage. For example, someone approaching the creation stories with a contextualist approach would recognize that the inspired author was using a mythic type of literature to teach that God is creator of all that is and that human beings have a responsibility toward God, creation, and other people. Given the literary genre, someone using this approach would not look for a scientific explanation in the story of how the world was created.

The Catholic church embraces and teaches the contextualist approach to the Scriptures, and, as mentioned above, it is used in *ScriptureWalk Senior High*. This approach to reading and interpreting the Scriptures requires more of the reader than does taking the stories literally, word for word, but it leads to more accurate and faithful interpretation. For more background on the contextualist approach, see the article in appendix A, "What the Scriptures Say . . . and Don't Say: Reading the Bible in Context."

Suggested Resources

An overwhelming number of resources for studying the Bible are available. We have reviewed many of them and recommend the following resources to leaders and groups using *ScriptureWalk Senior High*:

Achtemeier, Paul J., gen. ed. *HarperCollins Bible Dictionary.* [San Francisco]: HarperSanFrancisco, 1996. Provides helpful information on people, places, and concepts in the Bible.

Bergant, Dianne, and Robert J. Karris, gen. eds. *Collegeville Bible Commentary.* Collegeville, MN: Liturgical Press, 1989. Gives detailed information and interpretation for each book in the Bible.

The Bible Library for Catholics. Liguori Software, 800-325-9521. This computer CD-ROM has three complete Catholic translations of the Bible, Nave's Topical Index, search software, and more.

Kohlenberger, John R. III, ed. *The Concise Concordance to the New Revised Standard Version.* New York: Oxford University Press, 1993. Bible concordances show all the places selected words and themes can be found in a particular version of the Bible.

Ralph, Margaret Nutting. *"And God Said What?" An Introduction to Biblical Literary Forms for Bible Lovers.* New York: Paulist Press, 1986. A wonderful introduction to interpreting the Bible from a contextualist approach.

Singer-Towns, Brian. *The Bible: Power and Promise.* Winona, MN: Saint Mary's Press, 1997. This course from the Horizons series contains five sessions introducing the Bible. Use some or all of the course with your group before using *ScriptureWalk Senior High*.

Anger

Ephesians 4:25—5:2

Anger is a common and troubling emotion, not only for young people but for many adults too. We often seem to deal with anger with hurtful outbursts of angry words or violent actions. Or we submerge our anger and let it eat at us in unhealthy ways. However, the Bible calls us to embrace a healthy and virtuous response to anger: to acknowledge and even confront the situations that cause us anger but to avoid reactions that cause division, distance, and hurt. In this session we let the biblical vision challenge the young people to look for healthy ways to express their anger.

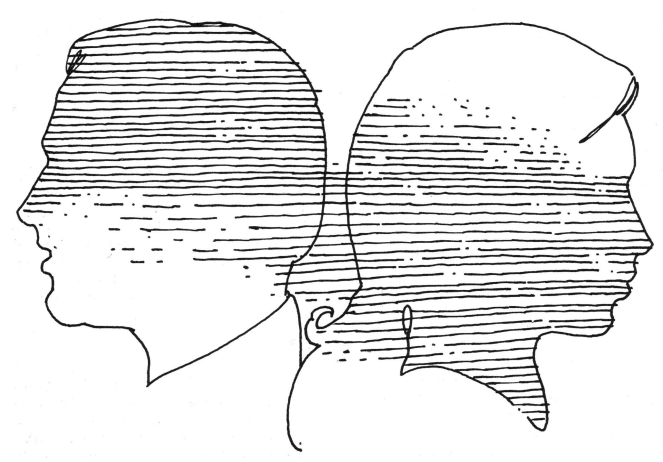

 # Study It

Healthy Responses to Anger (45–55 minutes)

Materials Needed

- ☐ Bibles, one for each person
- ☐ buttons of different sizes and colors, at least two for each person
- ☐ pens or pencils
- ☐ slips of paper, two for each person

Before the Session

- ☐ If you plan to have a student proclaim the Scriptures in step 2, tell him or her ahead of time so that he or she can practice.
- ☐ Decide how you will present the commentary in step 4 (see p. 12 of the introduction for options).

Step 1

Opening Activity (10 minutes)

Begin by explaining to the participants that this session is about anger and how Christian believers are called to deal with it. Add that the group members will look at their "anger buttons"—the things in life that tend to make them angry quickly, such as being caught in a traffic jam, being let down by friends who don't return repeated phone calls, or seeing someone mistreat a child. Share with them your own anger buttons.

Tell the young people to think of one or two of their own unique anger buttons, the things that really make them mad or get their goat. Pass out pens or pencils and a couple of slips of paper to each person. Instruct the participants to write one of their anger buttons on each slip. Explain that their responses will be shared with the group later.

After a minute or so, invite everyone to share what they wrote on each slip of paper. When all are done sharing, place an assortment of real buttons in the middle of the group and let everyone pick a real button as a symbol of the anger buttons they just shared. Tell them to hold on to their button for the rest of the session. Gather the slips of paper for use later in the session.

Step 2

Proclamation (5 minutes)

Invite the young people to think of the situation that their anger button represents as they listen to a reading from one of the New Testament letters describing what Christian community life should be. Direct the young people to open their Bible to Ephesians 4:25—5:2 so that they can follow along as the passage is proclaimed. When everyone is quiet and ready, proclaim Ephesians 4:25—5:2, or if you have asked a student to do so, instruct him or her to begin.

Step 3   Initial Reaction (10 minutes)

Lead a brief discussion using the following questions. If your group is large, break it into small groups of five to eight people for this step, if you haven't already done so. Have the group members refer to Ephesians 4:25—5:2 in their Bible, as necessary.

- What word or phrase from the passage stood out as you listened to the reading?
- Which line or verse seems to most challenge our society's way of handling anger? Why?
- Do most people you know handle anger in healthy ways? Explain.

Step 4   Commentary (5 minutes)

After the discussion, deliver the following commentary in the manner of your choice (see p. 12 of the introduction for options):

- This passage in the Letter to the Ephesians is part of a larger section giving advice on Christian living. The whole letter emphasizes Christian unity, and this particular passage calls on the readers not to allow sinful anger to divide the community. The author says it is okay to feel angry. Anger is a normal and appropriate human emotion—even Jesus felt it. The important thing is what we choose to do with our anger. The author says we should not allow the sun to set on our anger, which is a way of saying that we should not allow our anger to fester and build up to a level that might cause an outburst of extreme emotion or resentment. This is the point at which anger turns from a potentially constructive emotion to a potentially destructive one.

  The reading goes on to stress some practical and helpful ways to release our anger so that it does not get the better of us and turn destructive. The author advises us to be kind, honest, and forgiving of one another (4:32). These suggestions were probably as counter-cultural to the people of Ephesus as they are to us today. Forgiving a person who has hurt us has never been easy. It requires us to step back, to take a larger look at the situation from a different or more detached perspective. From that perspective, thoughts or comments like, "He did that on purpose because he hates me!" might change into questions such as, "I wonder what's causing him to do these things?" When this happens, it is easier to let go of hurt and bitterness and to move toward the virtues of kindness and forgiveness.

  In the Gospels Jesus often asks questions of people who challenge him or even accuse him of breaking the religious laws of his time. In this way he uses his anger for constructive change. His questions usually lead the other person toward conversion, that is, a change of heart. Remember the people who tried to trap Jesus by bringing him the woman caught in adultery? Instead of berating them for their mean-spiritedness, Jesus responded with an implied question, "Let anyone among you who is without sin be the first to throw a stone at her" (John 8:7). Or in the parable of the good Samaritan, instead of accusing his listeners of being narrow-minded or prejudiced, he asks, "Which of these three . . . was a neighbor to the man?" (Luke 10:36). Asking questions, rather than attacking or accusing others, is a good strategy for helping us to move beyond anger toward mutual understanding and, eventually, reconciliation.

A Christian's responses to angry situations should reflect those of Jesus. In the passage from Ephesians, the author concludes by asking us to "be like Christ." We are called to be "children of the light" and to shed light on the situations and feelings that are building up angry emotions within us. Speaking "the truth to our neighbors" (Ephesians 4:25) is a call not to ignore the things that make us angry but to address them in a positive way. Only then will we be able to let go of our anger, forgive those involved, and move on with the work of following Jesus. It is only through this ability to let go and forgive that we can control whether the sun will set on our anger.

Step 5 ## Application (15-25 minutes)

Use the following questions to involve the participants in further discussion on how Ephesians 4:25—5:2 applies to their life. You may wish to rephrase or add to these questions to tailor them to your group.

- Which stories from the Scriptures show Jesus being angry? What is the cause of his anger?

- How easily do you get angry? Do you tend to hold in your anger? Do you express it by getting even? Or do you try to reconcile with the other person and mend the relationship?

- Share an incident from the previous week when you were controlled by anger. Share a time when you controlled the anger. What made the difference in how you reacted to each situation?

- How hard is it for you to forgive people who have hurt you? Can you share a time when you forgave someone who hurt you deeply?

- What positive models for dealing with anger do we see in the media today? What negative models do we see?

- As a group create a list of ways for dealing with anger positively.

 # Live It

Anger Buttons (15–30 minutes)

This activity focuses on the choices we can make when situations provoke us to anger.

Materials Needed

☐ the buttons from step 1 of the Study It component
☐ the slips of paper on which the participants wrote their anger buttons from step 1 of the Study It component
☐ a box
☐ pens or pencils
☐ masking tape

Step 1

When doing this component as an independent activity. If you are doing this component independent from the other session components, you will need to have the young people fill out slips of paper with their anger button situations, as described in step 1 of the Study It component. Also, at the beginning of this step, you may want to proclaim Ephesians 4:25—5:2 and share the commentary in step 4 of the Study It component.

Direct everyone to put a piece of masking tape on both sides of their button and to write "Virtue" on one side and "Vice" on the other. While they are doing this, put all the slips of paper with the anger button situations in a box. When they are done, ask everyone to stand in a circle about an arm's length away from the person on either side of them.

Pass the box around the circle, directing everyone to each draw out a slip of paper. Select someone to begin and tell them to flip their button in the air. If it lands on the "Virtue" side, ask them to share a healthy, Christian response to the scenario on their slip of paper. If it comes up "Vice," they must suggest an unhealthy, sinful response to the same scenario. Feel free to gently challenge any response that you think is incorrect. Ask the group for alternate suggestions if needed.

After the person shares her or his response, everyone should take one step forward, toward the center of the group, if the response was healthy, or one step backward, away from the center, if it was unhealthy.

Moving around the circle in order, repeat this process until everyone has had an opportunity to go once. If you have time and if more scenario slips are in the box, start over with the first person.

Step 2 Ask the group members to look around the circle and connect hands with anyone they can reach without moving their feet. Invite them to comment on what they notice. It is hoped that they will observe that sinful responses to anger distance us from one another and create division; whereas healthy responses to anger bring us closer together.

Step 3 Summarize the previous exercise by saying something like the following in your own words:
- Life is like this exercise because it is often in the flip of a moment that we choose to respond to a situation in a healthy or an unhealthy manner. The more we are aware of our personal anger buttons, the better equipped we are to respond in virtuous ways when those buttons are pushed. In addition, the more we try to live out our faith, which is marked by the practice of forgiveness, the healthier all our anger responses will be and the less likely that the sun will set on our anger.

When doing this component as an independent activity. If you are using this component as an independent activity, you can extend it by having the group members brainstorm other situations that cause people their age to get angry. After listing these situations on newsprint, spend a few minutes discussing responses that would bring about a Christlike resolution to them.

Alternative Approach

Anger in the News
This alternative approach can replace the Live It component. Bring in newspapers from the current week and divide them among the participants. Tell them to find and cut out one or two articles about people responding angrily to some situation. When everyone is ready, invite them to share their findings with the group. For each article invite the participants to discuss the following questions:
- What are some healthy responses to the situation? What are some unhealthy responses?
- What effect did the people's angry response described in the article have on their family, their community, or other people involved? Could the outcome have been different? How?

After all the stories have been discussed, ask whether the majority of situations were resolved in healthy or unhealthy ways. Help the young people explore why that might be so.

Pray It

Forgiveness Meditation (15 minutes)

Materials Needed

- ☐ a candle and matches
- ☐ copies of handout 1–A, "The Prayer of Saint Francis," one for each person (or write the prayer out on newsprint for all to see)
- ☐ Bibles, one for each person
- ☐ a flashlight
- ☐ a tape or CD player, and a recording of reflective instrumental music (optional)

Prayer Directions

Begin by asking the young people to locate Ephesians 4:25—5:2 in their Bible. Set the mood for a quiet reflection by placing an unlit candle in the center of the group and darkening the room. Using a flashlight, read the following script slowly and prayerfully, pausing briefly at the ellipses (. . .). You may wish to play a recording of soft, instrumental music while you are reading the meditation.

Leader. When we speak or act in darkness, we speak and act alone.
[Light the candle.]

Leader. But when we speak or act in the light, we are never alone.
[Pause.]

Leader. Let us listen together, as children of the light, to God speaking to and through us.
[Instruct the group members to take turns reading one verse of the Scripture reading Ephesians 4:25—5:2. Designate who should begin. Pass a flashlight if needed. If you have more group members than there are verses, ask for volunteers to take turns reading the verses.]

Leader. Close your eyes and breathe deeply. . . . Relax. . . . Imagine that your entire life is being lived out in one full day. The sunrise brings with it your birth into a world full of wonder, mystery, and love. . . . With each hour that passes, you age another couple of years. . . . By midmorning you are beginning school . . . making friends . . . discovering the meaning of your feelings and emotions. . . . Pick a significant event that happened to you in your early childhood and relive it for a moment in your mind. . . .

As the afternoon begins, you enter the later years of childhood and begin your teenage years. . . . You experience many changes in your body . . . your friendships . . . and within your mind. . . . Think about an important event that occurred during your young teen years and reflect on it for a moment. . . .

As the afternoon wears on, you come to the last few hours of daylight . . . the last couple of years of your life so far. . . . Look over the last year, especially the last few months, and search out the people or situations that occupy your thoughts. . . . Focus on the people and events that have hurt you, that still tug at your emotions.

Anger •

. . . Silently name or picture in your mind one or two situations or people that still anger you.

As you keep these faces and situations in your mind, notice that the sun has started to set . . . that night is approaching, and with it darkness draws near. . . . You experience an urgency to work out the anger that controls part of you . . . to let go of the hurt that has been caused . . . to forgive the people who were involved. . . . You want to do this because you know it must be done before the sun sets . . . before darkness prevails. . . .

Spend a few quiet moments now with God. Talk to God about what you need in order to let go of the anger, the hurt, or the pride that is blocking you from the promise of peace. . . . *[Pause for a minute or two while individuals reflect.]*

As the sun gets ready to set, let go of the picture you have in your mind . . . let it drift away into the darkness. . . . Feel inside you the strength that returns after letting go of that heavy burden. . . . Enjoy the peace you now have in your mind. . . .

Slowly open your eyes and focus on the light of the candle that is before you. . . . Look deep within the light of the flame and see the God who gladly takes away the burden of your anger. Let God lighten the load of worry and concern from your mind. . . .
[If you wish, allow for a few minutes of spontaneous prayer or petitions. When the group members finish their prayers or petitions, pass out handout 1–A, "The Prayer of Saint Francis."]
Leader. Let us slowly say together the Prayer of Saint Francis.
[If necessary turn on the room lights for the participants to read the prayer. You may also invite them to sing the prayer.]
Leader. *[After finishing the Prayer of Saint Francis]* Let us conclude by sharing with one another a sign of peace.

Session Follow-Up

Family Connection

Invite the participants to take their anger button home and explain its symbolic meaning to their family. Suggest that they ask each member of the family to name two or three personal anger buttons—other family members can help out if someone gets stuck! Then tell them to encourage their family to talk about how they might help one another to respond in a healthy, life-giving way to each situation. Send home extra copies of handout 1–A, "The Prayer of Saint Francis," so the family can pray it together to end their sharing.

Daily Reading and Reflection

ScriptureWalk Bookmark
Distribute to the participants the bookmark for this session, found in appendix B. Point out that the bookmark has scriptural passages and questions on it. Invite the young people to deepen their understanding of the scriptural teaching on anger over the next several days by reading the passages and reflecting or journaling on the questions.

The Prayer of Saint Francis

Lord, make me an instrument of your peace.

Where there is hatred, let me sow love,

Where there is injury, pardon;

Where there is doubt, faith;

Where there is despair, hope;

Where there is darkness, light;

And where there is sadness, joy.

O, Divine Master, grant that I may not so much

    seek to be consoled, as to console,

    to be understood as to understand,

    to be loved, as to love.

For it is in giving that we receive,

    it is in pardoning that we are pardoned,

    and it is in dying that we are born to eternal life.

(David Schiller, editor, *The Little Book of Prayers,* pages 192–193)

Family

Exodus 20:1–12

Family relationships can be challenging for adolescents. Often a tension arises between their growing autonomy and the discipline of following family rules. This session invites the young people to look at the Ten Commandments as a starting point for understanding the connection between family rules and family relationships.

 # Study It

The Ten Commandments and Families
(45–60 minutes)

Materials Needed

☐ a sheet of poster board
☐ a marker
☐ Bibles, one for each person

Before the Session

☐ Prepare a poster of the Ten Commandments, using the wording from handout 2–A, "Family Commandments"
☐ If you plan to have a student proclaim the Scriptures in step 2, tell him or her ahead of time so that he or she can practice.
☐ Decide how you will present the commentary in step 4 (see p. 12 of the introduction for options).

Step 1

Opening Activity (10 minutes)

Ask each young person to share one of her or his family rules. For example, You have to call home if you're going to be late. Encourage participants to share different rules. List their rules on newsprint. After you have listed eight to ten rules, point to each one and ask for a show of hands to see how many people have the same rule in their family.

Optional activity: Parental cliches
As an alternative to step 1, have the participants call out the annoying sayings or cliches their parents use to chastise or correct them. For example: "If everyone was jumping off a cliff, I suppose you would too?" or "Stupid is as stupid does." Write their responses on newsprint. Young people find this exercise to be great fun, especially when they find out their friends' parents are saying the same things as their own.

Step 2

Proclamation (5 minutes)

Tell the young people that they are going to study a set of "family rules" that the Israelite people had with God. Direct the young people to open their Bible to Exodus 20:1–12 so that they can follow along as the passage is proclaimed. Ask them to keep in mind their own family rules as they listen to the reading. When everyone is quiet and ready, proclaim Exodus 20:1–12, or if you have asked a student to do so, instruct her or him to begin.

Step 3

Initial Reaction (10 minutes)

Lead a brief discussion using the following questions. If your group is large, break it into small groups of five to eight people for this step. In each group designate a discussion leader and give him or her a copy of these questions. Suggest that the group members refer to Exodus 20:1–12 in their Bible, as necessary.

- Which word or phrase from the passage stood out as you listened to the reading?
- Which commandment is most needed by our society today? Why?
- Which commandment is the most important one to you? Why?
- If you could add a commandment, what would it be?

Step 4   **Commentary (5 minutes)**

After the discussion deliver the following commentary in the manner of your choice (see p. 12 of the introduction for options):

- We often hear the Ten Commandments and think of them as a list of thou-shalt-not! warnings spoken in the deep, stern voice of God, like in the movies. What we may not realize is that these laws, though serious, are really the expression of the intimate love relationship between God and the Israelite people. Other ancient cultures had religious laws, but the Ten Commandments were unusual in their implied intimacy—most of the commandments begin with the word *you,* as though God were speaking directly to the Israelites. So rather than seeing the Ten Commandments as the demands of a controlling God, the Israelites saw them as a sign of God's special love for them.

  The Ten Commandments are also an important sign of the Covenant, that is, the mutual promises made by God and the Israelites to each other. God first established a covenant with Abraham, saying, "I will establish my covenant between me and you, and your offspring after you throughout their generations, for an everlasting covenant, to be God to you and to your offspring after you" (Genesis 17:7). God promised the Israelites, as the descendants of Abraham, to be their God—to love, protect, and remain close to them forever. For their part the Israelites promised to follow laws that would help them to know and love God and to live peacefully together. These laws are summarized in the Ten Commandments.

  The Ten Commandments appear in the Book of Exodus, but the Book of Exodus was written long after the actual events of the Exodus (Moses' leading the Israelites out of captivity in Egypt). The laws that are contained in the books of Exodus and Leviticus are the result of centuries of experience during which the Israelites learned about God, about human tendencies, about relationships between people. The tradition developed that God gave these laws all at once to Moses on Mount Sinai. This tradition created a dramatic story and emphasized the importance of the laws as an expression of the Israelites' love relationship with God. But the reality is that these laws were developed and refined over time as the Israelite people lived out their relationship with God and discovered what it meant to be a holy people.

  When we consider how the laws in Exodus came to be, the Ten Commandments can teach us several things about family rules and family relationships. First, family rules are an expression of the love that family members have for one another. They should remind us of what is important, keep us safe, keep things fair, and help us communicate well. Second, family rules should also be an expression of

the covenant—the mutual promises—that exist between parents and their children. The parents' promises are to nurture, teach, and keep their children from harm. The children's promises are to respect, obey, and learn from their parents. Finally, family rules, like the Israelite laws, grow and develop over time. Old rules may be modified or even dropped if the family members agree on a better way to live out their shared promises. Rules that applied when children were young have to change as they grow older and are capable of more responsibility.

Family rules can be a source of argument and controversy. However, if we use the Ten Commandments as our model for understanding the role and importance of family rules, they can be a lot easier to live with.

Step 5 — Application (15-30 minutes)

Use the following questions to involve the participants in further discussion on how Exodus 20:1–12 applies to their life. You may wish to rephrase or add to these questions to tailor them to your group.

- A covenant is a set of mutual promises between people in a relationship, for the good of everyone. What covenants are present between two parents? between parents and their children? between siblings?

- What did God want for the Israelites? How does this compare with what parents want for their children?

- Do you think parents make the best leaders of families, or should children be the leaders? How would your family life be different if the children were the leaders of the family?

- The Ten Commandments were meant, in part, to help keep order. Look at the rules you listed at the start of this session. How do they help keep order in family life? What would happen if these rules weren't there?

- What lessons have the members of your family learned about living peacefully together? How are these expressed in your family rules?

- Do any of your family rules need to be dropped or modified? Which ones? Why?

 # Live It

Family Commandments (15–30 minutes)

This activity focuses on living the Ten Commandments in the context of modern family life.

Materials Needed

☐ newsprint and markers
☐ masking tape
☐ copies of handout 2–A, "Family Commandments," one for every two people
☐ pens or pencils

Step 1

Have the group members name as many family problems as they can think of in 3 minutes. As they are calling out the problems, write them on sheets of newsprint. When 3 minutes are up, call time and ask the group to review the list. Circle any problems that they think are connected to the Ten Commandments and identify which commandments go with which problems. Some problems may be connected to more than one commandment.

Step 2

Divide the group into pairs (if you have an odd number of students, form one group of three). Distribute pens or pencils and give each pair a copy of handout 2–A, "Family Commandments." Assign each pair a different commandment from the left side of that handout. Direct the pairs to rewrite their assigned commandment in the space provided on the handout, using contemporary language and focusing on family relationships. For example, "You shall not bear false witness against your neighbor" might become "Brothers and sisters should be honest with one another and their parents." Let them spread out to work and give them several minutes to do this. When everyone is finished, call them back together.

Step 3

When doing this component as an independent activity. If you are doing this component as an independent activity, you may want to proclaim Exodus 20:1–12 and share the commentary from step 4 of the Study It component during step 3 of this activity.

Have each pair read their rewritten commandment aloud to the group and tell the group to guess which original commandment it is based on. Ask the group members if they think the rewritten commandment is true to the original version. If they don't think it is, let them suggest changes to help it be more faithful. Direct everyone to fill in the blank on their handout with the new family commandment.

Optional activity: Follow-up idea
When you are done, consider collecting these commandments and typing them up after the session. The list could be sent to the participants' families or put in a parish newsletter or bulletin to share the young people's work and to create awareness of the parish youth programs.

Step 4

Summarize the previous activity using the following points:
• The Israelites' relationship with God was similar to a family relationship. They followed certain expectations, or guidelines for living. The guidelines kept the peace and helped the Israelites learn and grow.
• The Ten Commandments helped the Israelites, but they also help us today.

When doing this component as an independent activity. If you are using this component as an independent activity, you can extend it with the following discussion starters:
• Make a list of different rules that families use to help them learn, grow, and live together in peace.
• Name some of the problems in our modern culture that might be prevented or solved if people more closely lived by the Ten Commandments.

Alternative Approach

Family Role-Plays
This activity is an alternative to the Live It component. Write down each one of the Ten Commandments on a separate slip of paper and place the slips in a bag. Split the group into pairs (and a group of three if necessary) and invite each pair to pick a commandment from the bag. Explain that each pair is to develop two short role-plays based on its chosen commandment:
• a family not living out the commandment very well
• the same family doing a good job in living out the commandment

Give the young people 10 to 15 minutes to work.

When everyone is ready, invite a pair forward to perform its role-plays for the entire group. Have the pair start with the role-play showing the family not living the commandment very well. Then ask the group for suggestions on how the family could live it out better. Then have the pair perform its second role-play to see how the partners worked it out. Repeat this process for each pair.

 # Pray It

My Family, My Self (15 minutes)

Materials Needed

☐ a mirror
☐ a piece of paper rolled up and tied with a ribbon (like a scroll)
☐ a bowl of M&M's or other small candies
☐ a crucifix or a cross
☐ four smaller candles (optional)
☐ a candle and matches
☐ writing paper
☐ pens or pencils
☐ a tape or CD player, and a recording of reflective instrumental music (optional)

Before the Session

Set up your prayer space by placing a different one of the following focusing objects in each of four corners of the meeting room: a mirror, a piece of paper rolled up and tied with a ribbon, a bowl of M&M's or other small candies, and a cross or a crucifix. Place the items on the floor or display them on tables. You may wish to place a small lit candle next to each item.

Prayer Directions

When everyone has arrived, dim the lights, light a candle, and place it in the center of the room. Gather the group members around the candle. Direct their attention to the items placed in the corners and explain that each item is a focusing object to help them reflect on and pray about their family relationships. Make the following observations about each item in your own words:

- The mirror can help you to focus on yourself and your own behavior and attitudes. As you look at the mirror, reflect on how well you are living your commitment to be a loving member of your family. Is there something you need to ask God's help with to live more peacefully with your family and enjoy them more? Go to this corner to pray about the things you can change about yourself.

- The M&M's can remind you of the sweet rewards of family life: the things you like to do together, the good memories you share, the lessons you have learned from family members. If you go to this corner, feel free to eat a piece of candy as you think about these things. Go to this corner to thank God for the good things about your family.

- The scroll can help you reflect on a covenant you have with your family. What promises have your family members made to one another as expressed in your family rules? Do these rules need to be modified? Maybe you could agree to do more around the house, and maybe your parents could give you a little more freedom. Maybe everyone could promise to try not speaking in anger, and waiting

until they are calm to address important issues. Go to this corner to pray about the changes you and your family could work on together.

- The cross [or the crucifix] can help you reflect on your family's faith life. Are you happy with the way your family lives out its beliefs? Do you pray together? Do you get involved in service to others? Go to this corner to pray about your family's faith life and how you could help make it grow.

Now hand out writing paper, and pens or pencils. Tell the young people they will have about 10 minutes to visit as many corners as they like. They are to do this in silence without disturbing anyone else. Ask them to write a reflection about each corner they go to. Suggest that they might want to compose a prayer or write down their thoughts and feelings as they reflect on each object. Explain that whatever they write is private, and they do not have to share it with anyone.

If you wish turn on a recording of reflective music. After about 10 minutes or when participants seem to be finished, call everyone back together. Ask them to repeat after you the following lines of the Serenity Prayer:

Leader. God grant me the serenity to accept the things I cannot change. *[Pause while the group repeats after you.]*

Leader. The courage to change the things I can. *[Pause while the group repeats after you.]*

Leader. And the wisdom to know the difference. *[Pause while the group repeats after you.]*

Leader. Amen. *[Pause while the group repeats after you.]*

Session Follow-Up

Family Connection

Invite the participants to talk to a grandparent or an older person in their parish about the family rules she or he had as a teenager. Have them ask how those family rules were different from the rules families tend to have today. Suggest that they ask this older person what he or she would be sure to include in "The Ten Commandments for Families Today."

Daily Reading and Reflection

Scripture Walk Bookmark

Distribute to the participants the bookmark for this session, found in appendix B. Point out that the bookmark has questions and scriptural passages on it. Invite the young people to deepen their understanding of the biblical teaching on families over the next several days by reading the passages and reflecting or journaling on the questions.

Family Commandments

In the space to the right of your assigned commandment or commandments, rewrite the commandment or commandments using contemporary language and focusing on family relationships.

The Ten Commandments

1. I am the LORD your God: you shall not have strange Gods before me.

2. You shall not take the name of the LORD your God in vain.

3. Remember to keep holy the LORD's Day.

4. Honor your father and your mother.

5. You shall not kill.

6. You shall not commit adultery.

7. You shall not steal.

8. You shall not bear false witness against your neighbor.

9. You shall not covet your neighbor's wife.

10. You shall not covet your neighbor's goods.

(*Catechism of the Catholic Church*, pages 496–497)

The Family Commandments

1. _____

2. _____

3. _____

4. _____

5. _____

6. _____

7. _____

8. _____

9. _____

10. _____

Forgiveness

Luke 15:11–32

There are times in most of our lives when we do not feel worthy of forgiveness. And there are times when we do not want to forgive someone else. Young people know these feelings too. In contrast to these feelings, Jesus' story of the prodigal son teaches us about God's incredible forgiveness. It challenges us to accept forgiveness and to extend it to others in the same radical way.

 # Study It

The Prodigal Son (45–60 minutes)

Materials Needed
- ☐ index cards, three for each person
- ☐ pens or pencils
- ☐ Bibles, one for each person

Before the Session
- ☐ If you plan to have a student proclaim the Scriptures in step 2, tell him or her ahead of time so that he or she can practice.
- ☐ Decide how you will present the commentary in step 4 (see p. 12 of the introduction for options).

Step 1

Opening Activity (10 minutes)

Welcome the group members and distribute to each person three index cards and a pen or pencil. Explain that you will read three stories out loud and that after each story the participants are to rate the likelihood of the story's ending in today's world. They should use a scale of 1 to 5, with 1 meaning not likely at all and 5 meaning very likely. Read each story below, and after each one give the participants a moment to write their rating on an index card. Then ask them to hold up their rating for everyone to see. Ask some volunteers to explain their rating. Avoid a long discussion, but if anyone rated the story's ending as unlikely, find out what they think might actually occur in the situation.

Story 1: The car wreck

A seventeen-year-old girl drives her father's new sports car without his permission, to show it to her friends. Driving recklessly to show off, she loses control of the car and wrecks it. When she is brought home by the police, her father embraces her and her mother prepares her favorite meal. The next morning the father takes her out and buys her a new car.

Story 2: The band contest

A group of friends who have formed their own band signs up for the high school talent show. The top prize is two hundred dollars and a chance to perform as an opening act at an upcoming concert. The lead singer, thinking that he can win the contest on his own, decides at the last minute to perform as a solo act and pulls out of the band. At the contest the band takes first place, and the lead singer takes third. He asks the group members if they will take him back to be part of the upcoming concert. The band agrees and even decides to highlight his name on the marquee at the concert hall.

Story 3: The prom date

John has dated Lisa for over six months and has already asked her to the prom. One month before the prom, John falls for Kristin, and sends a message to Lisa through a friend that he is going to take Kristin to the prom instead. Then one week before the prom, Kristin dumps John, and he is left dateless. John runs into Lisa at the mall and asks her if she would still go to the prom with him. Lisa, who had planned a beach trip that weekend with other friends, cancels the trip to go to the prom with John.

Step 2   Proclamation (5 minutes)

Explain to the group that you would like them to hear one more out-landish story of forgiveness that was told by Jesus. Invite them to consider what rating the people listening to Jesus might have given the end of the story.

Direct the young people to open their Bible to Luke 15:11–32 so that they can follow along as the passage is proclaimed. When everyone is ready, proclaim Luke 15:11–32, or if you have asked a student to do so, instruct him or her to begin.

Optional activity: Character assignments
Given the length of this Luke passage, you may wish to divide it into the following five parts and select people in the group to read each part: Jesus (narrator), the father, the younger son, the older son, the servant.

Step 3   Initial Reaction (10 minutes)

Lead a brief discussion using the following questions. If your group is large, break it into small groups of five to eight people for this step. Have the group members refer to Luke 15:11–32 in their Bible, as necessary.
- Which word or phrase from the passage stood out as you listened to the reading?
- What character in the story did you most identify with? Why?
- Of all the things the younger son did wrong, what would have been most difficult for you to forgive if you were the father? if you were the older brother?
- What believability rating, on a scale from 1 to 5, would you give this story if you were one of Jesus' listeners? Why?

Step 4   Commentary (5 minutes)

After the discussion deliver the following commentary in the manner of your choice (see p. 12 of the introduction for options):
- To fully understand the significance of this particular parable, we need to understand the laws and customs of Jesus' time. Then we can really appreciate how Jesus pulled the rug out from under his audience and challenged peoples' assumptions about who God is and how God judges people.

In this story Jesus is responding to the Pharisees and scribes who were grumbling about Jesus' spending time with sinners (Luke 15:2). The first thing they hear is that a younger son is insulting his father by asking for his inheritance while his father is still alive. The Pharisees and scribes would have been shocked by the son's behavior because by Jewish custom an inheritance could not be spent until after the father's death. This immediately set up the younger son as the "bad guy" in the story.

Next, the younger son misuses his money through sinful living. His hunger during the famine would have been seen as a just punishment for his total disregard for his religious, familial, and cultural roots. When he tends the pigs to keep from starving, it is a sign that he is lost forever, because pigs were considered unclean by Jewish law.

By now the audience is probably thinking that the point of Jesus' story is to illustrate what happens to Jews who break with the law and tradition—that God will justly punish them for their sinfulness. So with perfect timing, Jesus shocks the scribes and Pharisees by presenting a radically different ending from what they were expecting.

The son, relinquishing his pride, decides to try to return to his father's household as a mere slave. Even this was taking a chance, because Jewish custom required a father to publicly disown a son who had behaved so badly, shunning all contact with him and treating him as a nonperson. Instead, the father does exactly the opposite in welcoming his son back:

- The father runs to greet his son—even though social custom considered it undignified for an older person to run.
- The father embraces the son—even though the son was considered unclean because of his association with pigs. By hugging the son, the father makes himself unclean, and as the audience hears this, they are, in effect, being "grossed out."
- The father kisses the son—this is a biblical sign of forgiveness and probably the last thing the audience expects the father to do to this boy.
- The father calls for shoes to be given to the son—shoes were for freemen only; slaves went barefoot.
- The father gives him a ring and robe to wear—these were signs of royalty and authority. This person who broke all the rules and disobeyed authority is being raised to an esteemed level.
- The fatted calf is killed and a celebration held—this type of party was reserved for significant people and would have drawn everyone's attention to the father's taking the sinful son back. The party told the whole village of the "foolishness" of both father and son.

As the Pharisees and scribes hear Jesus tell of these outrageous actions by the father, we can imagine it made it harder and harder for them to accept Jesus' story. When the angry older son is introduced, they probably immediately identified with him as the only rational Jew in the family. So the father's final words to the older brother are also Jesus' words to the Pharisees and scribes: "You are always with me, and all that is mine is yours. But we had to celebrate and rejoice, because this brother of yours was dead and has come to life; he was lost and has been found" (15:31–32).

Jesus is calling the scribes and Pharisees—and us—to come to terms with the radical nature of God's love and forgiveness. It simply does not make sense . . . unless you are the one needing forgiveness. The story of the prodigal son reminds us that God is wildly in love with us, and it models how we are called to forgive one another as well as ourselves.

Step 5   Application (15-30 minutes)

Use the following questions to involve the participants in further discussion on how Luke 15:11–32 applies to their life. You may wish to rephrase or add to these questions to tailor them to your group.

- What keeps most people from asking for forgiveness? from offering forgiveness to people who have wronged them?

- Can you name any action or person that God would not forgive? Why do you think this is so?

- What is the most difficult step in the process of forgiveness?

- What are some ways people avoid forgiving another person? What happens as a result?

- The young son hit rock bottom when he tended the pigs and ate their food. What would you say has been the lowest point in your life? Where was God during this time? Who or what helped you up again?

- Have you ever experienced a radical and transforming act of forgiveness like that of the younger son? Can anyone share that experience with the group?

- Have you ever experienced anger over an act of forgiveness that seemed unfair? Can anyone share that experience with the group?

 # Live It

The Great Cereal Feast (20–30 minutes)

This activity focuses on the burden that we carry when forgiveness is not taking place and shows how letting go of the hurt or hate can free us to live and love more fully.

Materials Needed

☐ a table
☐ a couple of boxes of a popular cereal, new and sealed
☐ a carton of milk
☐ spoons, one for each person
☐ cereal bowls, one for each person
☐ masking tape
☐ newsprint and markers
☐ pens or pencils
☐ blank sheets of 8½-by-11-inch paper, ten to fifteen sheets for each person and a few extra

Before the Session

☐ On a table across from where the young people will gather, place a carton of milk, a couple of boxes of a popular cereal (new and sealed), and enough cereal bowls and spoons for everyone.
☐ Using masking tape on the floor, mark off a starting line that is about 10 yards away from the table.
☐ Hang a sheet of newsprint in the meeting area.

Step 1

When doing this component as an independent activity. If you are doing this component independent from the other session components, at the beginning of this activity, you may want to proclaim Luke 15:11–32 and share the commentary in step 4 of the Study It component.

Gather the participants and have them brainstorm a list of "young people's laws," that is, rules that young people would agree are important for good relationships with others and with God. You might want to share a couple of examples such as the following:
• Do not gossip about others.
• Be honest with your parents.
• Treat your boyfriend or girlfriend with respect.

    Invite someone to be a scribe and give him or her a marker with which to list each law on the newsprint. Encourage the young people to make an exhaustive list, covering family life, friendships, school, jobs, religion, driving, and so on.

Step 2   Give each person ten to fifteen sheets of paper and a pen or pencil. Tell the participants to write on each sheet of paper a different young people's law that they have broken or that someone else broke at their expense. Assure them that they will not be asked to reveal what they wrote on their papers. Instruct them to crumple up each paper after they write on it and keep it in front of them. Distribute additional sheets as needed, reminding the participants to write only one law per sheet.

Step 3   When everyone has finished writing, explain that their assignment is to hold all their crumpled sheets in their hands while they go over to the table, pour themselves a bowl of cereal and milk, and then eat it. The only catch is that if they drop any one of their crumpled papers, they must sit down wherever that paper drops and remain there until further instructions are given.

Have the participants go one at a time, beginning with the person who has the most pieces of paper. Explain that everyone must at least try to start, sitting down whenever they drop their first piece of paper. At that point the next person attempts to get to the cereal, avoiding the people who are sitting in her or his way. Emphasize that the crumpled sheets must be held in the hands and cannot be carried in a shirt or squeezed under the arms. If you see anyone doing this, they must stop and place all the papers in their hands or sit down where they are. The idea is to make it impossible for anyone to perform the assigned task. Even if they do make it to the table, they will not be able to pour milk and eat while holding their papers.

Once everyone in the group has tried and failed, explain that you will now forgive their first effort and offer them a second chance to successfully eat a bowl of cereal. And best of all, this time they get to leave their pieces of paper behind, right where they fall. Then invite all the participants to get a bowl of cereal and sit around the table to eat together.

Step 4   As everyone is eating their cereal, discuss the following questions with them:
- What feelings did you experience when you made your first attempt at getting a bowl of cereal?
- What did the papers symbolize to you? How is carrying them around similar to how we carry our hurts and guilt around with us in life?
- Why do we insist on trying to hang on to hurts, sins, and anger? Why is it so difficult to let go and forgive others?
- How does this story relate to the prodigal son passage? Who in the story is carrying their "papers," and who has let go of them?
- What is God inviting us to do with our hurt, our failures, our anger, and our shortcomings in order to join in God's great feast?

Alternative Approach

Happily Ever After

This activity is an alternative to the Live It component. Explain to the group that fairy tales are somewhat similar to parables because they were created to help people understand a certain value or bit of cultural wisdom. Note, however, that most fairy tales differ from parables in that they follow an expected course where the hero or heroine saves the day and ends up living happily ever after.

Tell the group that you want to challenge them to redo the ending of a popular fairy tale so that it resembles a parable. Just as Jesus' parables did, their fairy tale parables should pull the rug out from under the listeners' feet. Their endings should emphasize radical love and forgiveness and should be a surprise to anyone who is familiar with the way the fairy tale is usually told.

Divide the group into teams of three to four people and have each team select a popular fairy tale. Some fairy tales they might use are Sleeping Beauty, Rumpelstiltskin, Snow White, Jack and the Beanstalk, Cinderella, Little Red Riding Hood, and Goldilocks and the Three Bears.

Once each group has selected a fairy tale, give everyone 10 minutes to rewrite the ending. Tell the teams that when time is up, they can either tell their fairy tale parable to the group or act it out.

When time is up, have each team present its fairy tale parable to the group. After each presentation, lead the group in a discussion using the following questions:

• What new values or rules does this new version teach?
• What might happen if this story were told and retold over the years to children throughout the world?

Pray It

Letting Go of Your Burdens (15 minutes)

Materials Needed
- ☐ a large trash bag
- ☐ the crumpled papers from the Live It activity
- ☐ a candle and matches
- ☐ a tape or CD player, and a recording of reflective instrumental music (optional)
- ☐ Bibles, one for each participant
- ☐ a copy of the act of contrition from the end of this prayer service (or a piece of newsprint or poster board on which you have written it for all to see)

Before the Session
Set up the prayer space by placing the large trash bag in the middle of the meeting area, surrounded by all the crumpled pieces of paper from the Live It activity.

Prayer Directions
When doing this component as an independent activity. If you are doing this component independent from the other session components, begin by proclaiming Luke 15:11–32, the parable of the prodigal son. Hand out blank pieces of paper, and pens or pencils. Ask the young people to write on each of eight to ten pieces of paper the name of a different person who has hurt them or a person they have hurt. Tell them to crumple up these sheets of paper and throw them around the trash bag. Emphasize that no one will see what they have written on these papers.

Gather everyone around the trash bag, light the candle, and place it near the trash bag. If you wish turn on a recording of reflective instrumental music.

Explain that the trash bag represents God and the crumpled papers represent the burdens of our sins and hurts. Tell the young people that as you read the following prayer, you will be inviting them at four different times to pick up a few of the crumpled papers near them and deposit them into the trash bag as a sign of their willingness to turn their sins and hurts over to God.

Leader. If you believe in a God who cannot stop loving you, no matter what, then let go of your own hatred and hurt and place some of your burdens, represented by these papers, in the trash bag. *[Pause.]*

Leader. If you believe in a God who died for you on the cross so that your sins may be forgiven, then let go of the sins that are weighing you down and place some more of your burdens in the trash bag. *[Pause.]*

Leader. If you believe in a God who ate with sinners and healed those who were broken, then let go of the guilt and hurt that you have been carrying around with you and place some more of your burdens in the trash bag. *[Pause.]*

Leader. If you believe in a God who could forgive a son who turned his back on all his family and religious values, then show your belief that God can do even more wondrous things with you by placing your remaining burdens in the trash bag. *[Pause.]*

Leader. Now extend your hands over the trash bag as we offer a prayer of reconciliation to God.

Act of Contrition

Everyone. God of infinite forgiveness, you love us so deeply that you are willing to forgive all our sins, heal all our hurts, and overlook all our shortcomings.

It is hard to believe that you could be so wildly in love with us. We need your help to live in the freedom your love brings to our lives. Accept these pieces of paper as a symbol of our desire to seek forgiveness from those we have hurt and of our desire to reconcile with those who have hurt us.

Be with us as we go forward this day knowing that you walk with us and are always willing to reconcile us to you whenever we stray from you. We ask this through Christ, our risen and saving Lord. Amen.

Leader. I now invite each of you to offer one another a sign of Christ's peace and forgiveness.

Session Follow-Up

Family Connection

Invite the participants to share the prodigal son reading, Luke 15:11–32, at home with their family. Make copies of the following directions to send home with them:

Read aloud the story of the prodigal son in the Bible, Luke 15:11–32, and discuss the following questions:
- Which character in the story of the prodigal son can you most relate. Why?
- Tell a story of a time when you were forgiven like the younger son. How did it feel?
- Is there anything needing reconciliation within your family now? If so, talk about it.

Close the sharing with a time of prayer for peace and forgiveness. Invite each family member to share her or his own prayer for the family.

Daily Reading and Reflection

Scripture Walk Bookmark
Distribute to the participants the bookmark for this session, found in appendix B. Point out that the bookmark has questions and scriptural passages on it. Invite the young people to deepen their understanding of the biblical teaching on forgiveness over the next several days by reading the passages and reflecting or journaling on the questions.

Friendship

Sirach 6:5–17

For adolescents, friends are as necessary as food and water. However, many young people discover that friendship can be painful as well as life-giving. This session uses a passage from the Book of Sirach—part of the Old Testament wisdom literature—to study what true friendship is. The book's author, Ben Sira, emphasizes that true friends are a special gift, and must be chosen carefully.

 # Study It

True Friendship (45–60 minutes)

Materials Needed

☐ newsprint
☐ markers, one for each person
☐ bumper sticker–size pieces of paper or poster board
☐ masking tape
☐ Bibles, one for each person (make sure you have Catholic Bibles, which include the Book of Sirach)

Before the Session

☐ Write the following two sentence starters on a sheet of newsprint:
 ○ A faithful friend is . . .
 ○ Friendship is . . .
☐ If you plan to have a student proclaim the Scriptures in step 2, tell him or her ahead of time so that he or she can practice.
☐ Decide how you will present the commentary in step 4 (see p. 12 of the introduction for options).

Step 1   **Opening Activity (10 minutes)**

Pass out to each person a piece of bumper sticker–size paper or poster board, and a marker. Tell the participants that they are each to create a bumper sticker with a unique slogan on friendship. The slogans may be based on the sentence starters displayed on the newsprint, or they may be some other creative expression about friendship.

Give the group about 5 minutes to work. Then have each person share his or her bumper sticker with the whole group. If possible tape the bumper stickers on the walls of the room.

Step 2   **Proclamation (5 minutes)**

Tell the young people that they are going to look at a passage from the Bible that teaches about true friendship. Direct them to open their Bible to Sirach 6:5–17 so that they can follow along as the passage is proclaimed. When everyone is ready, proclaim Sirach 6:5–17, or if you have asked a student to do so, instruct her or him to begin.

Step 3   **Initial Reaction (10 minutes)**

Lead a brief discussion using the following questions. If your group is large, break it into small groups of five to eight people for this step. In each group designate a discussion leader and give him or her a copy of these questions. Have the group members refer to Sirach 6:5–17 in their Bible, as necessary.

• What word or phrase from the passage stood out as you listened to the reading?
• Which verse would you use on a bumper sticker or a T-shirt?

Friendship

- Is there anything in the passage that sounded harsh to you? What was it?
- What is God saying to us in this passage about friends?

Step 4

Commentary (5 minutes)

After the discussion deliver the following commentary in the manner of your choice (see p. 12 of the introduction for options):

- The word *friend* is a lot like the word *love*. We use it all the time without thinking about its true meaning or significance, and yet it's probably one of the most important words in our language. Friendship plays a vital role in our life, all through our life. Ben Sira, the author of the Book of Sirach, knew this and had learned the importance of choosing his friends wisely.

  The Book of Sirach (or Ecclesiasticus) is part of the wisdom literature of the Old Testament, or Hebrew Scriptures. The wisdom books also include Job, Psalms, Proverbs, Ecclesiastes, the Song of Solomon, and the Wisdom of Solomon. Instead of dealing with historical events in Israel's history, the wisdom books reflect on life's mysteries. They deal with themes like the meaning of life, why good people suffer, and what makes a person wise. The teachings in Sirach are drawn from the experience of Ben Sira, a wise teacher who lived about two centuries before Christ. Reading this and other passages from Sirach is like sitting and listening to a grandparent's advice: the words may sound like stern warnings meant to frighten us, but they really are loving advice given to protect and ensure our happiness.

  The warnings about false friends in the first half of the Sirach passage might seem harsh or even mistrustful. But Ben Sira knew the dangers of false friends. He lived in a time when the Jewish people were under Greek domination. The Greeks were proud of their culture and probably did not think much of Jewish culture or customs. Some of the Jews of Ben Sira's time were eager to be friends with the Greek rulers, to obtain wealth or importance for themselves. They embraced Greek customs and culture, abandoning their Jewish friends and families. Such people caused a lot of hurt in the Jewish community.

  We, too, know that some people choose friends based on the status it gives them, or even the access to money and power. But people are not things to be used. Nor are people conveniences to be tossed aside when they have served their purpose or become burdensome. This is what Ben Sira saw, and this is what he warned against. We must never be people who use and abandon others, and we must be alert not to be used and abandoned ourselves by false friends.

  Through Ben Sira, God teaches us that true friends stand by us in good times and in bad times. Interestingly, in verses 8 and 10, the phrase "stand by you" (or "be with you") is a phrase that is also used to describe God's presence with the Chosen People. The way a friend stands by us in times of trouble is the same way God stands by his chosen ones. In a very real way, when we experience true friendship, we experience God.

46

Step 5   Application (15-30 minutes)

Use the following questions to involve the participants in further discussion on how Sirach 6:5–17 applies to their life. You may wish to rephrase or add to these questions to tailor them to your group.

- Based on this passage, how would you define friendship?

- The first half of the Sirach passage warns about fair-weather friends. Have you ever had the experience of trusting someone too soon? Why should we be concerned about false friends?

- Ben Sira counsels, "Let those who are friendly with you be many, / but let your advisers be one in a thousand" (6:6). What do you think he means by that?

- Have you ever had a friend who was like a sturdy shelter or a life-saving medicine? Talk about him or her.

- Ben Sira lived in a time when the Jewish people were in danger of not living their faith fully, to be more acceptable to their Greek friends. How does your choice of friends affect the way you live out your Christian faith?

- Verse 16 says "those who fear the Lord" will find faithful friends. What is the connection between having a relationship with God and having faithful friends?

 # Live It

Spin-the-Bottle Dear Ben (20–30 minutes)

This game takes the advice given about friendship in Sirach 6:5–17 and connects it with everyday experiences. It is best done in groups of five to eight young people.

Materials Needed

☐ empty 2-liter plastic bottles, one for every five to eight participants
☐ copies of resource 4–A, "Game Cards for Spin-the-Bottle Dear Ben," one for every five to eight participants
☐ a pair of scissors

Before the Session

☐ Cut apart the game cards from each copy of resource 4–A so that you have one identical set of cards for each small group.

Step 1

When doing this component as an independent activity. If you are doing this component independent from the other session components, at the beginning of this step, you may want to proclaim Sirach 6:5–17 and share the commentary in step 4 of the Study It component.

Have participants sit in circles of five to eight people, and place an empty 2-liter plastic bottle and a set of game cards from resource 4–A in the middle of each circle. Ask the young people to open their Bible to Sirach 6:5–17 to refer to during the game.

Explain that they are going to play spin the bottle a little differently than it is traditionally played. It's actually going to be a combination of spin the bottle and an advice column. The game begins with the youngest person in each group picking a game card and reading it aloud. The card asks Ben Sira for some advice on a friendship situation. After reading the question, the person spins the bottle. The person the bottle points to when it stops spinning must give the advice asked for on the game card. The adviser should try to give advice that reflects Sirach's wisdom, but in his or her own words.

If someone has trouble thinking of appropriate advice, they may ask the group for help. And after each response, the group members should give their reaction to the advice. Do they think it would work? Is there anything they would add? Is it really what Ben Sira would say?

Step 2

When you are done explaining the game, begin playing. After each person's turn, continue playing by having the person who gave the advice read the next card and spin the bottle. The person must keep spinning the bottle until it points to someone who has not had a chance to give advice yet. Each person in the small group must have a turn at giving advice in response to at least one card before anyone else in the group gets a second chance.

Step 3   If you have time, after all the groups are finished, ask each group to share with the large group one piece of advice that it really liked. Summarize the activity by putting the following points into your own words:

- There are several levels of friendship. On one level, friends are the people whom we know by name, see occasionally, and have casual conversation with. On a deeper level, friends are the people whom we see more often—the people we work, study, or socialize with. At the deepest level, friends are the few, close friends with whom we can talk about our innermost feelings and important decisions. A balanced person has friends at all levels.
- For someone to develop a friendship at the deepest level takes time and commitment. We should be careful of letting someone in at that level too quickly or too easily.
- To have friends at that deeper level is truly a blessing. As Ben Sira says, "Whoever finds one has found a treasure" (Sirach 6:14).

Alternative Approach   **Friendship T-Shirts**
Have all the participants bring an old, plain white T-shirt to the session (men's undershirts work great). Or you could ask people in the parish to donate some. Direct the young people to use fabric markers, pens, or paints to make their own friendship T-shirts.

There are at least two different ways to create the shirts. One way is to have each person decorate their own shirt, writing on it slogans from the friendship bumper stickers (if you did that activity from the Study It component) and phrases from Sirach. The second way is to have the whole group decorate the shirts together. Instruct everyone to write on their shirt their name and a short slogan on friendship based on the advice given in Sirach. Then tell them to pass their shirt around the group and have each person write his or her slogan on it and initial it. This is probably the most fun and memorable way to create the friendship T-shirts.

The young people can keep their friendship T-shirt and use it as a nightshirt or wear it to other youth activities.

 # Pray It

Thank You, Friend (15 minutes)

Materials Needed

☐ Bibles, one for each person
☐ a candle and matches
☐ pens
☐ lined paper, at least one sheet for each person
☐ a tape or CD player, and a recording of songs about friendship (such as Michael W. Smith's "Friends," James Taylor's "You've Got a Friend," or Natalie Merchant's "Trouble Me")

Prayer Directions

Gather everyone in the prayer area and light a candle. Begin by inviting one of the young people to proclaim Sirach 6:14–17. Explain that through this Scripture passage, God is telling us just how special good friends are. Then hand out lined paper and pens and ask the young people to write a letter to thank a friend for his or her friendship. It could be someone their own age, or a family member, a coach, or a teacher who has been a friend to them. Tell them to include the qualities of that person that make the friendship special. They might want to include any lessons they have learned about friendship from that person. While they are writing, play some quiet instrumental music or a few songs about friendship.

After 5 minutes ask the young people to finish their letter in the next few minutes. When all are finished, ask them to read their letter silently to themselves, but to read them now as if they had written it to Jesus.

When the young people are done reading, ask them to silently reflect on the following questions:

• What would you change in the letter if you were really writing it to Jesus?

• How is the friend you addressed in the letter a sign of Jesus' presence in your life? Do you feel that you have a relationship with Jesus as a close friend? If not, why not take a moment and tell Jesus you want to have a close relationship with him.

Invite the young people to take a few minutes to pray silently or out loud for their friends and about their friendship with Jesus. When the shared prayer is done, invite the young people to join hands in a circle and bring to mind the friend they wrote the letter to as you close with the following prayer:

• God of faithfulness, we ask your blessing on these friends of ours. And if anyone is in need of a friend, please bring opportunities for friendship into that person's life. Help us to also be faithful friends, and most of all help us to remember your friendship and your faithfulness. We pray in Jesus' name. Amen.

Session Follow-Up

Family Connection

Instruct the participants to ask a parent or a grandparent for his or her advice on friendship, based on personal experience. Suggest that the young people share the Sirach 6:5–17 passage with the parent or grandparent and ask his or her thoughts on it. Also suggest that they ask the person about his or her oldest or best friend and share a story about what that friendship has taught him or her.

Daily Reading and Reflection

Scripture Walk Bookmark

Distribute to the participants the bookmark for this session, found in appendix B. Point out that the bookmark has questions and scriptural passages on it. Invite the young people to deepen their understanding of the scriptural teaching on friendship over the next several days by reading the passages and reflecting or journaling on the questions.

Game Cards for Spin-the-Bottle Dear Ben

Make a photocopy of this resource for each small group of five to eight participants. Cut apart the Dear Ben letters so that each group has a set of ten game cards.

Dear Ben,
I have a large group of friends, and we share everything. We don't have any secrets from one another, but lately a lot of things I've said to these friends are being repeated around school. What should I do?

Dear Ben,
I like to get together with my friends to party and have a good time. But I don't like it when they start getting serious on me. So whenever that happens, I always joke around to get them to lighten up. Now they're telling me that I have to get serious sometimes. Should I look for a new group to hang out with?

Dear Ben,
I always like to show new friends right away that I trust them. I loaned my favorite jacket to a new friend, and now it's lost. Isn't it right to trust people?

Dear Ben,
The person I thought was my best friend is now my worst enemy. We got in a huge argument, and now it's getting blabbed all over school that I'm the mean one! Should I do the same thing to her?

Dear Ben,
It takes a long time for me to get close to a friend and really feel like I can trust him or her. Is that bad?

Dear Ben,
I have a couple of friends who only seem to come around when I can get the car. I feel like they're using me. What do you suggest I do?

Dear Ben,
I'm jealous of my sister. She seems to have tons of friends. I only have a few. Should I try to be more fun so that I can get more friends?

Dear Ben,
I like to be around people who make me look good and feel good. If someone starts getting too negative, I'm out of there. People think I'm being shallow, but I say I'm just being smart—I've got enough problems of my own without getting involved in someone else's problems. What do you think?

Dear Ben,
One of my friends and I go to church together. We're in the same youth group too. I spend just as much time with my other friends, but I feel closer to this person than to my other friends. Why is that?

Dear Ben,
A while ago I was really close to someone who suddenly cut me out of his life. It hurt me terribly. I made a vow that I would never let someone do that to me again. It's not worth the hurt to let someone get that close to you, is it?

Hope

Psalm 31:1–16

This session looks at how hope can help young people through situations, emotions, and concerns that may lead them into despair. The author of Psalm 31 also knew hopeless times, times when "those who see me in the street flee from me" (verse 11). Like the psalmist, we must learn to find our hope by putting our trust in God, who is "my rock and my fortress" (verse 3).

 # Study It

Hope in Hopeless Times (45–60 minutes)

Materials Needed
- ☐ blindfolds, one for every two people
- ☐ M&M's or other small pieces of candy, one for each person
- ☐ Bibles, one for each person (The Bibles need to be the same version for step 2.)

Before the Session
- ☐ Decide how you will present the commentary in step 4 (see p. 12 of the introduction for options).

Step 1

Opening Activity (10 minutes)

Direct the participants to pair up (if you have an odd number of students, form one group of three), and give a blindfold to each pair. Tell the group members that you are going to put them in the most hopeless situation you can think of: Due to a terrible accident, they have a broken leg and are blinded. They have been stranded alone without food for three days. They must find some food or starve.

Tell the participants that in order to do this simulation, each partner must take a turn being the blinded, lame, starving person. Have the oldest person in each pair put on the blindfold. Explain that when you tell the blindfolded people to begin searching for food, they may only hop or crawl, because of their broken leg. Give a piece of candy to each of the people who are not blindfolded and tell them to hide it somewhere in the room where it cannot easily be found. Then tell the blind, lame, hungry survivors to start searching for the candy. Assure them that their partner will keep them from bumping into things or people, and from taking another pair's candy.

Allow a couple of minutes of frustrated searching. Then tell the nonblindfolded group members to place a hand on the shoulder of their partner and silently and gently guide her or him to the candy. Wait until each person has found her or his piece of candy. Then have the partners switch roles and repeat the process.

When everyone has finished, ask the group members to consider these questions silently:
- How did you feel when you were blind, lame, and starving with no one to help you? helpless? hopeless?
- How did you feel when you felt the strong hand of a silent presence helping you? What could that presence symbolize in the life of a Christian?

Step 2   **Proclamation (5 minutes)**

Note: For this reading to work, everyone will need to read from the same Bible version.

Tell the young people that the people of Israel had many experiences of hopelessness. They suffered through many wars, conflicts, and times of poverty. Together you are going to read part of Psalm 31, which expresses some of these feelings.

Have everyone find Psalm 31:1–16 in their Bible and read the passage aloud with the group. Ask those who were blindfolded first to read the odd-numbered verses and the others to read the even-numbered verses. Remind them to read the verses slowly, trying to get in touch with the feelings and emotions being expressed through the words.

Step 3   **Initial Reaction (10 minutes)**

Lead a discussion using the following questions. If your group is large, break it into small groups of five to eight people for this step. Have the group members refer to Psalm 31 in their Bible, as necessary.
- Which word or phrase from the psalm stood out as you listened to it?
- Could young people today identify with any of the emotions or verses that were contained in this reading? Which ones?
- If you could offer one sentence of advice to the person in this psalm, what would it be?

Step 4   **Commentary (5 minutes)**

After the discussion deliver the following commentary in the manner of your choice (see p. 12 of the introduction for options):
- The reading we just heard is called a psalm and is found in the Old Testament Book of Psalms. Psalms are poetic prayers to God written by the ancient Israelites. There are 150 psalms recorded in the Book of Psalms, and others are sprinkled throughout the Scriptures. Psalms are divided into several types, including psalms of praise, psalms of thanksgiving, psalms of worship, wisdom psalms, and psalms of lament. Psalms like Psalm 31 teach us that it is okay to complain or cry out to God in fear, anger, or confusion. Other psalms teach us to shout for joy and sing out in praise of God. In short, psalms teach us how to pray and converse with God in both the good times and the bad.

  Psalm 31 is a psalm of lament. Psalms of lament were prayed to recover the experience of shalom, or peacefulness, that was missing for some reason from a person or a community. It is no coincidence that the majority of the psalms found in the Scriptures are either individual or communal laments. After all, the Israelites had been through many wars, battles, and exiles over their long history. What is surprising is that despite these crises, these psalms still express the Israelites' belief in a God who would help them out of these seemingly hopeless and helpless situations. Throughout their history, the Israelite people had witnessed God's saving actions time and time again. These experiences gave them hope that God would not abandon them in their times of need.

Psalm 31 is about an individual who seems to be at rock bottom in life. The psalmist (the one making this prayer) feels "spent with sorrow" (verse 10) and thinks that his neighbors ignore and gossip about him (verses 13–14). The person feels alone, isolated, and hurt. The psalmist's only hope is to trust in God, his "rock and fortress," the only one who can free him from his depression and isolation.

Young people express these same feelings and thoughts today, especially during difficult experiences like when their parents divorce or they fail at something really important. When we have nothing to hope in but ourselves, these experiences can be truly devastating. But Psalm 31 shows us another way. We can put our trust in God, who surrounds us and lifts us up, especially during the darkest moments. What a comforting and saving image to bring peace to our fear, strength to our weakness, and hope to our despair.

Psalms allow people today to know that their fears and depressions, concerns and anxieties, and hopes and joys are not unique. These emotions have been expressed by people of faith over the centuries to God, who is present and active in our world. This insight can offer comfort and hope to us that our God is a God who can be spoken to, who does hear our petitions, and who will not abandon us in our time of need. This is the Good News and the source of our hope.

Step 5 **Application (15-30 minutes)**
Use the following questions to involve the participants in further discussion on how Psalm 31 applies to their life. You may wish to rephrase or add to these questions to tailor them to your group.

- Verse 9 speaks about being delivered into "enemy hands." What enemy hands are young people today being led into? How do these situations create an atmosphere of hopelessness in the world of some young people?
- Is it difficult for people to trust in others, including God, during the tough times of life? Why or why not?
- Think of one of your most hopeless times in life and share the verse in Psalm 31 that best reaches to the depths of those feelings. Describe this to the group.
- Which phrase or verse would have given you the most hope during that particular time in your life? Why?
- What are some ways to give hope to another? What have others done to give you hope?

 # Live It

Hope Sculptures (15–30 minutes)

This Live It component focuses on an experience of hopelessness that the young people have encountered in their life and what helped give them hope during that particular time.

Materials Needed

☐ 12-by-12-inch sheets of aluminum foil, two for each person
☐ drawing paper
☐ markers

Step 1

When doing this component as an independent activity. If you are doing this component independent from the other session components, at the beginning of this step, you may want to proclaim Psalm 31:1–16 and share the commentary from step 4 of the Study It component.

Distribute a 12-by-12-inch sheet of foil to each person. Instruct everyone to reflect on a time in their life when they felt hopeless, hurt, and alone. As they recall the situation, and the feelings associated with it, invite them to create a symbolic sculpture out of their foil that best depicts this experience for them. (If participants cannot work with the foil, give them some paper and markers, and have them draw or write something that symbolizes the experience for them.)

Give them about 5 minutes to complete their sculpture. When everyone has finished, go around the group and have each person share his or her work and the story behind it with the rest of the group.

Step 2

When the first round of sharing is finished, distribute a second sheet of foil and, if necessary, paper and markers, and direct the participants to create a sculpture symbolizing who or what gave them hope during this hopeless time in their life. Again, give them about 5 minutes to complete their work, and when everyone has finished, let each person share his or her sculpture, drawing, or written work, and the meaning behind it.

When doing this component as an independent activity. If you are doing this component as an independent activity, you may wish to conclude by discussing the following questions with the group:

• During these times of difficulty and hopelessness, where was God? How do you know?
• What would you do if someone shared with you that they saw no way out of their problem or situation and did not feel like dealing with it any longer?
• What resources in your parish, community, and schools exist to get help for those who feel helpless or hopeless?
• What are the signs of hope and hopelessness right now in your life?

Alternative Approach

Symbols of Hope and Hopelessness

Collect and display in the middle of the group several objects that might symbolize hope, such as a strong branch, a rock, a heart cutout, a flower, seeds, a lit candle, and a Bible. Also gather and display objects that might be interpreted as signs of hopelessness, such as a spent candle, a torn cloth, a broken or cracked mirror, and a dying flower or weed.

Gather everyone around the display and invite them to each select one object that best symbolizes despair and hopelessness to them and to share why. Encourage them to relate it to a story of hopelessness that occurred in their life. After all the participants have shared, lead a discussion of the following questions:

- During these times of difficulty and hopelessness, where was God? How do you know?
- What piece of wisdom or advice would you offer to other people who find themselves in hopeless situations?
- What would you do if someone shared with you that they saw no way out of their situation and did not feel like dealing with it any longer?

After everyone has finished, ask them to each select another object from the table, this time one that best symbolizes hope and trust. Again, have them explain why. Ask them to try to connect a personal experience to their explanation. When the stories of hope have been shared, lead a discussion of the following questions:

- How would you describe hope, in five words or less?
- What prevents young people from feeling hopeful today?
- How does your faith offer you hope?

 **Pray It**

Trusting God (15 minutes)

Materials Needed

- ☐ a baby blanket or some other type of soft blanket
- ☐ the foil sculptures (and drawings or written works) from the Live It activity (optional)
- ☐ a candle and matches
- ☐ slips of paper
- ☐ pens or pencils
- ☐ Bibles, one for each person
- ☐ a tape or CD player, and a recording of a song about hope (such as Gloria Estefan's "Coming Out of the Dark" or Amy Grant's "Hope Set High") (optional)

Before the Session

Place a baby blanket on the floor in a circle as if a pet might come and sleep on it. Put the foil sculptures (and drawings or written works) created in the Live It activity in the middle of the blanket, being sure that room is left around the edges for the blanket to be folded over all the objects.

When doing this component as an independent activity. If you are doing this component independent from the other session components, just leave the blanket empty.

Prayer Directions

Invite everyone to sit in a circle as you light the candle next to the blanket on the floor. Explain to the participants that as Psalm 31 is read out loud, they are to reflect on an experience, person, or situation that is on their mind now and that is causing them or someone they know to feel hopeless and hurt. Ask them to open their Bible to Psalm 31, then going around the circle, have each person read one of the verses, through verse 16. When finished, invite everyone to take their slip of paper and pencil and write down whatever hopeless situation or person is occupying their thoughts right now.

After a couple of minutes of silence, tell the group that the blanket on the floor represents God, who is there to hold us with our despair and fears, comforting us just as we would comfort a small baby. As a symbol of the young people's willingness to let go and allow God to take care of them, invite them to place their slips on the blanket, one person at a time.

When all the slips of paper have been placed on the blanket, take the ends of the blanket and fold them over the papers and foil sculptures so that they are hidden from the group's view. As you do this, tell them that it is now God's turn to take on these concerns and cares and it is our job to let go of them and to trust in the goodness and love of God. If you have chosen a reflection song about hope, play it and ask the young people to listen to its message.

Conclude the prayer by inviting everyone to join hands and say the Lord's Prayer together.

Session Follow-Up

Family Connection

Option 1: Affirmation letters
Invite the young people to write a note of affirmation to a family member who gave them hope during the past year. Suggest that in their letter they explain to the person they are writing to how he or she offered them hope and helped them out of a low or difficult time in their life. If there is time, let them write more than one letter.

Option 2: Table discussion
Encourage the young people to invite their family to gather together and read Psalm 31:1–16. Have the family members share with one another a story about a hopeless time in their life and how they overcame it. They could also talk about how their faith in God was a source of strength to them in difficult times. Suggest that the family conclude their time together by sharing messages of hope or affirmation with one another.

Daily Reading and Reflection

Scripture Walk Bookmark
Distribute to the participants the bookmark for this session, found in appendix B. Point out that the bookmark has questions and scriptural passages on it. Invite the young people to deepen their understanding of the biblical teaching on hope over the next several days by reading the passages and reflecting or journaling on the questions.

Love

1 Corinthians, Chapter 13

Love is one of the most widely used—and perhaps misused—words in the English language. This session looks to Saint Paul's First Letter to the Corinthians for a better understanding of what defines real Christian love, namely, that it is other-centered and not self-centered. The young people will look at this type of love and how it can transform their ordinary gifts and relationships into extraordinary ones.

 # Study It

Real Love (45–60 minutes)

Materials Needed

☐ enough copies of resource 6–A, "Scrambled Phrases," so that you have a numbered section for each pair
☐ a pair of scissors
☐ pens or pencils
☐ Bibles, one for every person
☐ newsprint
☐ masking tape

Before the Session

☐ Cut apart each copy of resource 6–A along the dotted lines.
☐ Post a sheet of newsprint on the wall.
☐ If you plan to have a student proclaim the Scriptures in step 2, tell him or her ahead of time so that he or she can practice.
☐ Decide how you will present the commentary in step 4 (see p. 12 of the introduction for options).

Step 1

Opening Activity (10 minutes)

Divide the group members into pairs (if you have an odd number of students, form one group of three) and give each pair a pen or pencil and one of the scrambled phrase slips from resource 6–A. It's okay if you don't hand out all the phrases or if you use the same phrase for more than one pair.

Explain that they have been recruited to become code breakers and that you have just received a coded message from somewhere in the Middle East. Tell the participants that each pair has a phrase from the total message. Their mission is to unscramble their phrase, write it correctly on their slip, and tape or glue it in the proper order with every other pairs' phrase on the newsprint that you have posted on the wall. All the phrases together will reveal the secret message.

Stress to the participants that time is of the essence and that they have only 2 minutes to perform this task. In order not to confuse the various phrases, explain that it is important to not talk to the other pairs while working on their own scrambled phrase.

Some phrases are missing the word *love* and, therefore, cannot be fully unscrambled. If group members ask whether all the words are present, just tell them that you don't have any other information at the moment.

After 2 minutes ask each pair to read the part of its phrase that is unscrambled. If the pair has been unable to unscramble anything, simply ask them to read the phrase as it appears on the slip of paper. Do not allow discussion or questions, but go quickly from pair to pair, having each one read out loud its phrase. If any pair has successfully unscrambled its phrase by adding the word *love,* simply tell those people that they have an interesting theory.

Step 2   **Proclamation (5 minutes)**

Announce to the group members that you just received new information that their phrases were incomplete and that you now have a missing key word required to complete them. Ask if anyone has any idea what the key word is. Tell them that headquarters has supplied a code book—their Bibles—and they should turn to 1 Corinthians, chapter 13, for help in unscrambling their phrase. Once they have unscrambled their phrase, they should write it on their slip and tape it in the proper order on the newsprint. Note that you will not have phrases for all the verses in the chapter because some of the more difficult ones were not used.

When they have finished, direct the young people to open their Bible to 1 Corinthians, chapter 13, so that they can follow along as the Scripture passage is proclaimed. Proclaim chapter 13, or if you have asked a student to do so, instruct him or her to begin.

After the reading, share with the group that this session is about the topic of love and the important role it plays in the lives of those who choose to follow Jesus. Much like their work with the phrases themselves, people often try to solve the puzzle of life without this type of love.

Step 3   **Initial Reaction (10 minutes)**

Lead a brief discussion using the following questions. If your group is large, break it into small groups of five to eight people for this step. Have the group members refer to 1 Corinthians, chapter 13, in their Bible, as necessary.

• What is your favorite line or phrase from this passage?
• Who or what do you think of when you hear this reading?
• What did you hear in listening to this passage that you didn't notice before? Why did it strike you?

Step 4   **Commentary (5 minutes)**

After the discussion deliver the following commentary in the manner of your choice (see p. 12 of the introduction for options):

• Although today chapter 13 of 1 Corinthians is often chosen by couples for their wedding, Paul had a much different audience in mind when he included this section in his first letter to the people of Corinth nearly two thousand years ago. At that time it was a stern warning to the community about what real Christian love is all about. In the chapters before this passage, we learn that certain leaders are holding their special role or gifts above others in a competitive way to appear more favored by God. Paul calls this an abuse of the charisms, or gifts, that God has graciously given these leaders for the good of the community.

In order to straighten out this crooked thinking, Paul reminds the Corinthians that if any gift is to serve God, it must reflect an unselfish, other-centered love—the same love that Jesus modeled in his life. This other-centered love is the key—and sometimes the missing ingredient— that turns an ordinary talent into an extraordinary gift. Gifts and talents that are used in the name of God for selfish reasons end up being worthless. But any gift—no matter how big or small—when used for the good of others will shine forth brilliantly.

We probably have all encountered the braggart who possesses a particular talent, but cannot stop talking about it and telling everyone how special he or she is. This self-praise actually lessens or cheapens the gift, as well as the person who possesses it. This is not the other-centered love that Jesus calls his followers to live out.

To drive home his point, in verse 11 Paul reminds us that as we grow to adulthood, we put childish ways aside. He implies that those whose love is self-centered have yet to experience mature love. We would hardly want to love others the same way as an adult as we did when we were three years old. Paul challenges the Corinthians—and us—to keep growing in our understanding of love. How can we know and experience the fullness of our totally self-giving God if we have not grown to understand and practice unselfish love? It may take us a lifetime to get there, but the result is worth the effort.

Step 5   Application (15-25 minutes)

Use the following questions to involve the participants in further discussion on how 1 Corinthians, chapter 13, applies to their life. You may wish to rephrase or add to these questions to tailor them to your group.

- Why is it that many people have a difficult time understanding this Christian ideal of love?

- Give an example from the popular media (movies, songs, magazines, television) of self-centered love.

- Saint Paul's life story serves as a good example of an extraordinary gift being transformed by the love of God. His hatred and persecution of Christians was totally turned around through his own experience of God's unselfish love. Share a story of someone you know who was changed by an experience of other-centered love.

- If Paul were writing this letter to young people today, how might he complete the following statements to challenge us to live out this unselfish, Christian love:
  Love is . . .
  Love never . . .
  Love is not . . .

- Could living this type of other-centered love change or transform the different relationships you are in right now? For example, could it change your relationship with your best friend? with a friend of the other sex? with a parent? with a coworker? with God? If so, how?

- Invite everyone to select one phrase or verse from 1 Corinthians, chapter 13, that reflects a strength they have as a loving person and share it with the group.

- Invite everyone to select one phrase or verse from 1 Corinthians, chapter 13, that most challenges them in becoming a more loving person and share it with the group.

 # Live It

Many Colors, One Picture (15–30 minutes)

This Live It activity focuses on how we are each given gifts for the common good and not our own glory. It is best done in groups of five to eight young people.

Materials Needed
- ☐ different-colored markers, enough so that each person in each small group has a different color
- ☐ drawing paper, one sheet for each person
- ☐ two sheets of newsprint
- ☐ masking tape
- ☐ prizes (for example, large candy bars), two for each small group of five to eight people

Before the Session
Write the following list on a sheet of newsprint and post it where everyone can see it:
- a tree
- a bird
- the sun
- some hills
- a flower
- a dog
- a stream
- fish

Step 1
Form small groups of five to eight people each. Give each young person in a group a different-colored marker (using colors appropriate to the items you listed on the newsprint) and a piece of paper. Explain to everyone that they are going to have an art contest. Assign each person in a group a different object from the list on the newsprint that you posted. Give the following directions for the contest:
- Everyone must draw their assigned object, using only the marker they possess right now. No one may share markers.
- Each small group will name a contest winner from within its group. The winner will be determined by a group vote and will receive a prize [hold up prizes of your choice, for example, large candy bars]. However, the winner must receive at least half the votes of the group. The prize may not be shared.
- You will have 5 minutes to draw your picture.

Step 2
After 2 minutes have the participants share their drawing with the rest of their small group. They can attempt to persuade others to vote for their drawing. Direct the groups to cast votes by raising hands. If there are any winners (more than half the votes of the small group), give each of them a prize and remind them that it may not be shared with anyone in the group. If there are no winners (no one in any small group got enough votes), put the prizes away.

Step 3   Explain to the young people that they are about to work on another drawing, but the rules will be slightly different this time. This drawing will still include only the objects listed on the newsprint and each person still may only use the marker that was given to him or her. The difference is that the members of each team will work on the same piece of paper, creating one drawing for each small group. Supply each group with a sheet of newsprint or poster board and explain that it has 5 minutes to draw a group picture.

When time is up, tell the young people that each person must compliment someone else's part of the drawing. Allow each person to do this. Award any remaining prizes to the entire group.

Step 4   *When doing this component as an independent activity.* If you are doing this component independent from the other session components, at the beginning of this step, you may want to proclaim or have someone else proclaim 1 Corinthians, chapter 13. You may also wish to read the commentary in step 4 of the Study It component.

Summarize by making the following points, in your own words:
- Paul says that our individual gifts, no matter how great, are worthless if they are used selfishly, without love.
- The colored markers represented our individual gifts. With only one color, the picture we could create was limited. In the same way, when we use our gifts only for ourselves, our life will be limited.
- When we combined the markers, a more creative and colorful picture could be drawn. In the same way, when we share our gifts with one another, our life and the lives of other people in our families and communities will be richer and more fulfilling.

If you have time, continue the activity by leading a discussion of the following points, in your own words:
- What happened to this group when the participants bragged about their drawings and listened to others brag?
- What happens when we hide or do not share our gifts? What is our motivation to share our gifts?
- What made step 3 more like the love Paul describes?

Alternative Approach   **Valentine Love**
Display on a table Valentine cards or candy hearts with different sayings on them. Invite the young people to each choose one they would like to receive. Have everyone share what they chose and why.

If you have not read chapter 13 of 1 Corinthians, do so now. Then ask the young people if they would like to trade in their Valentine for the type of love that is expressed in this reading. Follow this with a discussion based on the following questions:
- What do these Valentine messages say about the way love is often understood in our culture?
- How are these Valentine messages like Paul's definition of love? How are they different from Paul's definition of love?
- How well do we as a society live out the challenging kind of love Paul describes? How could we do better?

 # Pray It

Prayer of Love (10–15 minutes)

Materials Needed
- ☐ two copies of the prayer script in this component
- ☐ a Bible
- ☐ a candle and matches
- ☐ a mirror
- ☐ a tape or CD player, and a recording of a song about unselfish and transforming love (optional)

Before the Session
- ☐ Recruit two volunteers to be readers for the prayer service and give them each a copy of the prayer script so that they can look over their part. While they are doing this, place a candle and a small mirror in the prayer area and open a Bible to 1 Corinthians, chapter 13.

Prayer Directions

When you are ready, light the candle, dim the lights, and lead the group in the following prayer, based on 1 Corinthians 13:4–8:

Leader. God of love, you created us in love while your Son, Jesus, showed us by his life and by his death what true love is all about. We come to you in prayer now and recognize that you are here with us. *[Pause.]*

Reader 1. Love is patient.

Reader 2. Help us to be patient, Lord, especially when it is difficult. Give us the strength to stay calm when tempers flare or those around us seek to annoy and provoke.

Reader 1. Love is kind.

Reader 2. Help us to show your love in our actions.

Reader 1. Love is not envious or boastful or arrogant or rude.

Reader 2. May we always seek to unite and not to divide, to help and not to hurt.

Reader 1. Love does not rejoice in wrongdoing, but rejoices in the truth.

Reader 2. May we always seek honesty in others and ourselves.

Reader 1. Love never ends.

Reader 2. We ask you to make us aware of the things that last and the things that don't.

Leader. I invite you to pray out loud now for the people, relationships, or struggles that need God's unconditional love. Our response to each prayer will be, "Lord of love, heal us."
[Allow time for shared, spontaneous prayer.]

Reader 1. When I was a child, I spoke like a child, I thought like a child, I reasoned like a child; when I became an adult, I put an end to childish ways.

Reader 2. We are no longer children; help us to become the people you call us to be.

Reader 1. For now we see in a mirror dimly, but then we will see face-to-face.

Reader 2. And now faith, hope, and love abide, these three; and the greatest of these is love.

[If you have selected a song, play that now.]

Leader. May the God of all love continue to bless us, our gifts, and our relationships so that we may better live out unselfish and other-centered love all the days of our life. We ask this through Christ our risen Lord. Amen.

Session Follow-Up

Family Connection

Suggest that the students try the following activity at home. Make copies of the directions to send home with the participants.

Make heart cutouts with white paper. Set out pens, markers, and crayons on a table. Gather the family members around the table. Ask everyone to write their name on a heart and then pass it to the left. Everyone is to write or draw on the heart that is passed to them something they really love about the person whose name is on the heart cutout. When everyone is done, pass the hearts to the left again and repeat the process until each heart has been drawn or written on by everyone. Consider turning on some music during this process (let each child in the family choose one of his or her favorite songs).

When all are done, spend a few minutes reading the comments out loud and talking about them.

Daily Reading and Reflection

ScriptureWalk Bookmark

Distribute to the participants the bookmark for this session, found in appendix B. Point out that the bookmark has questions and scriptural passages on it. Invite the young people to deepen their understanding of the scriptural teaching on love over the next several days by reading the passages and reflecting or journaling on the questions.

Scrambled Phrases

Make enough photocopies of this resource so that you have a numbered section for each pair. The numbers represent verses from 1 Corinthians 13:1–8,13. Cut apart each copy along the dotted lines, for use in step 1 of the Study It component.

----

1.   clanging cymbal   not have   if I speak in   angels, but do
     I am a noisy   the tongues of   gong or a   mortals and of

----

2.   understand all mysteries   I have prophetic   and if
     powers and   and all knowledge   remove mountains,
     I am nothing   but do not have   all faith so as to
     and if I have

----

3.   away all my   I gain nothing   I hand over
     that I may boast   possessions and if   but do not have
     if I give   my body so

4–5. irritable or resentful   way it   is kind   or boastful or
     is not envious   it does not   is patient   arrogant or rude
     insist on its own   is not

----

6.   in wrongdoing   in the truth   but rejoices
     it does not rejoice

----

7.   hopes all things   all things   It bears
     endures all things   believes all things

----

8.   but as for prophecies   Love never ends
     it will come to an end   as for tongues
     they will come to an end   they will cease   as for knowledge

----

13. abide these three   hope and   and the
     and now   faith   these is   greatest of

Prejudice

Luke 10:25–37

Young people are very aware of prejudice in its many forms. But like many adults, they may think that prejudice is someone else's problem. The parable of the good Samaritan in the Gospel of Luke is Jesus' attack on the sin of prejudice, pointing out a wrong, but socially accepted, cultural prejudice among the Jews. This session will help the young people understand the challenge for them in the question, Lord, who is my neighbor?

 # Study It

Who Is Your Neighbor? (45–60 minutes)

Materials Needed

☐ a copy of resource 7–A, "Scrambled Scripture Story"
☐ Bibles, one for each person

Before the Session

☐ If you plan to have a student proclaim the Scriptures in step 2, tell him or her ahead of time so that he or she can practice.
☐ Decide how you will present the commentary in step 4 (see p. 12 of the introduction for options).

Step 1 **Opening Activity (10 minutes)**

Ask for the group's help in completing the story on resource 7–A, "Scrambled Scripture Story," but don't give any clues about the nature of the story. Before reading the story, solicit the students' input for each blank in the story by naming the type of phrase required (see the bracketed phrase below each blank line). After they have called out several responses for the first blank, write in the response that will yield the silliest reading. Continue in this manner until each blank is filled in.

Then ask for a volunteer to read the story. After everyone has had a good laugh, ask if anyone can name the Scripture parable that the story is based on.

Step 2 **Proclamation (5 minutes)**

Tell the participants to think of a group of people that everyone distrusts and that gets blamed for much of what is wrong in the world. Then ask them to imagine that this group is called the Samaritans and to keep this in mind during the Scripture proclamation. Direct them to open their Bible to Luke 10:25–37 so that they can follow along as the passage is proclaimed. When everyone is ready, proclaim Luke 10:25–37, or if you have asked a student to do so, instruct him or her to begin.

Step 3 **Initial Reaction (10 minutes)**

Lead a brief discussion using the following questions. If your group is large, break it into small groups of five to eight people for this step. Have the group members refer to the Luke passage in their Bible, as necessary.

• What word or phrase from the passage stood out as you listened to the reading?
• Describe the kind of person you think of when you hear the phrase "good Samaritan."
• In Jesus' time who would have been upset by hearing this?

- If you were the person who had asked Jesus, "Who is my neighbor?," how would you have reacted to his answer?

Step 4   **Commentary (5 minutes)**

After the discussion deliver the following commentary in the manner of your choice (see p. 12 of the introduction for options):

- The story of the good Samaritan is a parable. A parable uses everyday events and images to teach a lesson or illustrate a point. The parables told by Jesus usually had unexpected endings that surprised his listeners. Jesus used parables to teach, to comfort, and to challenge his audiences. The parable of the good Samaritan is one of the challenging kind. In it Jesus lets his followers know that there is no room in the Kingdom of God for prejudice or hate—that every single human being is our neighbor.

   To understand this parable, we must know that Samaritans were looked down on by Jews of Jesus' time. This prejudice had its roots centuries earlier, when Samaritans married non-Jews. They also didn't keep the Jewish laws exactly as prescribed by the priests and scribes, so their religion was seen as a polluted form of Judaism. With this in mind, let's take a closer look at the story.

   For several reasons Jesus' listeners may have excused the seemingly heartless lack of action by the priest and the Levite (Levites were Temple servants and officials). First, the man who gets attacked in the story was leaving Jerusalem to go to Jericho. This was widely known to be a dangerous route infested with robbers and Jewish Zealots who preyed on travelers. Jesus' listeners may have been thinking, "This guy shouldn't have been traveling alone in the first place—he deserved what he got." Second, it was common for a robber to fake an injury to lure a victim closer. Who could blame the priest and the Levite for not taking any chances? Finally, if the priest or the Levite stops and touches a wounded person, according to Jewish religious laws, he will be contaminated—made unclean by exposure to the man's blood—and therefore unable to perform his Temple duties. Helping this man could result in a loss of income to him.

   At this point the listeners might expect a lay Jewish man to be the hero, thinking that the lesson of Jesus' story is the hypocrisy of religious leaders. Instead, Jesus delivers his surprise ending—the hero is from a group they despise: the Samaritans. A person who is supposed to have no understanding of the Law is the only one to fulfill the core command of the Law: "to love your neighbor as yourself." Jesus' Jewish audience would have found this ending offensive, maybe even outrageous. It is doubtful that they would have thought of it as an enjoyable story about a nice man helping someone in need.

   To be fair, the Law as stated in Leviticus 19:18 defines one's neighbor as a fellow Israelite. But some of the prophets from the Old Testament had taught that God is the God of all people. Jesus is following in that tradition. In one seemingly simple story, he clearly affirms that to love your neighbor means to love all people—not just those who share your cultural and religious background. This is the challenge for us today as well.

Just like Jesus' Jewish audience, we can think of ourselves as free from all prejudice. But it is never as simple as that. It is easy to be blind to our own prejudices. They might be revealed in that uneasy feeling we have around people from another race, or in the jokes we tell that make fun of another culture. They might be reflected in our attitude toward poor people or rich people. They might be in the gossip we share with our friends about people in other groups. However our prejudices are reflected in our life, exposing and rising above them is an important and lifelong task for Christians.

Step 5   **Application (15-30 minutes)**
Use the following questions to involve the participants in further discussion on how Luke 10:25–37 applies to their life. You may wish to rephrase or add to these questions to tailor them to your group.

- Jesus used parables to teach truths. What truth is being taught in the parable of the good Samaritan?

- Have you ever experienced discrimination or prejudice? How did it make you feel?

- Do you believe all people possess prejudices of some sort? What are some of the more common ones today?

- How can someone uncover their prejudices, especially if those prejudices are part of their family or community life?

- What prejudices do you have? What kind of people are you nervous or uncomfortable around?

- What steps can you take to rise above your own prejudices, like the good Samaritan does in helping an "enemy"?

 # Live It

Me? Prejudiced? (20–30 minutes)

This Live It activity uses the characters from the good Samaritan story to help the participants look at their own prejudices. It is hoped that this self-examination will help them understand who God might be calling them to see as their neighbor.

Materials Needed

☐ newsprint and markers
☐ masking tape
☐ pens or pencils
☐ writing paper

Before the Session

☐ At the top of a sheet of newsprint, write "Powerful person (Levite)," on another sheet write "Respected person (priest)," and on a third sheet, "Despised person (Samaritan)." Post the three sheets in the meeting room.

Step 1

When doing this component as an independent activity. If you are doing this component independent from the other session components, at the beginning of this step, you may want to proclaim Luke 10:25–37 and share the commentary in step 4 of the Study It component.

Ask the participants to consider the labels on the newsprint that you posted and to think of groups or categories of people, both adults and youth, that fit into these categories today. Offer an example for each category, such as a banker as a powerful person, a teacher as a respected person, and a gang member as a despised person. (If your group members need thinking time, you might distribute pens or pencils, and paper and let them do this exercise individually.) Have them call out the names of as many groups or categories of people as they can think of. Record their responses on the appropriate sheet of newsprint.

Ask the participants to use names that are not insulting or derogatory—that is, to name the groups or categories with the same respect that they would like people to use in naming them.

Step 2

Divide the group members into teams of three to six people each, making sure that you have at least three teams. Give each group pens or pencils, and writing paper. Assign one of the following tasks to each team. If you have more than three teams, assign one or more of the tasks to more than one team. Give the young people 15 minutes to work. Tell everyone to be ready to share their assignment and responses with one another.

- *Task 1.* As you look at the list of despised people, talk about why they are disliked. Then list as many ways that you can think of to overcome these reasons. For example, if a group is despised because of other people's ignorance, that obstacle might be overcome by having the people who are uneducated about the group learn more about or spend time with the group members.
- *Task 2.* Choose a group or category from each list to replace the characters in the good Samaritan parable. Rewrite the parable in a modern setting or prepare a short skit based on the parable using these new characters.
- *Task 3.* Consider the lists of respected people and powerful people. Make a list of things these people could do to reduce prejudice in your community. Make a list of things you could do.

Step 3   After 10 to 15 minutes, gather the groups together and ask each group to share its assignment and responses. Conclude by making the following points in your own words:
- Prejudice continues to exist in today's world, sometimes in subtle ways, sometimes in overt ways.
- There are many reasons for prejudice, but they all have the same root cause—the unwillingness to see another person or group of people as members of God's family.
- If we accept that all people are also children of God, then we have to accept them as our equals in God's eyes, sharing our full humanity with all the strengths and flaws that we are prone to.

If you have time, or if you are doing this component as an independent activity, you could conclude by discussing the following questions:
- Why is it so easy to develop and hold on to prejudices?
- How does prejudice affect Christians and the Christian faith?
- What commitments can your group make to weeding out prejudice in itself?

Alternative Approach

A Collage on the Theme, Who Is My Neighbor?
Tell the group members that they will be creating collages on the theme, Who is my neighbor? You can have them do this individually or in groups of two to four, depending on the size of your group and the supplies you have available. Have on hand glue, paper or poster board, and a supply of magazines with pictures of diverse people. Make sure various ages, sizes, races, styles of dress, and so on, are represented in the magazines. Give the young people about 15 minutes to work.

After the participants have finished their collage, lead a discussion with questions like the following:
- Why did you choose the pictures that you did?
- What kind of prejudices are associated with the different types of people in your collage?
- Do you have personal examples of those prejudices to share?

 # Pray It

Healing Prejudice (15 minutes)

Materials Needed

☐ a Bible
☐ one long elastic bandage, 24 to 30 inches of bandage for every participant (you may need to connect several bandages together)
☐ fabric pens, one for each person
☐ a candle and matches
☐ a tape or CD player, and a recording of reflective instrumental music (optional)

Before the Session

☐ Ask a volunteer to prepare to read Luke 10:25–37.
☐ Make a circle on the floor with a long elastic bandage (24 to 30 inches of bandage for each participant) and tie the ends together so the circle is complete. Place an unlit candle in the center of the circle.

Prayer Directions

Give each participant a fabric pen and ask everyone to sit in a circle around the bandage that you have prepared. When you are ready, light the candle in the center of the circle and call the group to prayer.

Leader. Let us now listen again to the words of Jesus, challenging us to put aside all our prejudices and stereotypes and embrace all people as our neighbors.

Reader. [Read Luke 10:25–37.]

Leader. I invite you now to bring to mind the people you know who are the Samaritans in our own community, the people who are hated and ridiculed by others. They can be a clique, an ethnic group, a class of people, or particular individuals. As you think of these modern-day Samaritans, write on the bandage the titles, categories, or first names of these people.

[Allow a few minutes for the group members to think and write. If you like, play reflective instrumental music. After everyone has written something, ask the participants to hold the bandage in their hands and stand, maintaining the circle.]

Leader. Just as the Samaritan bandaged the Jew, his enemy, we are called to heal and be healed by our own enemies. We pray now that we might see every person as our neighbor. I invite you to take turns saying the names or words you wrote on the bandage. After each one is called out, let us all respond, "We pray that we might love them as we love ourselves."

[After each response, have the person who just spoke wrap the bandage once around his or her wrist. After everyone has taken a turn, have them step away from the center to pull the bandage tight. Then make the following points in your own words:]

Leader. This bandage, a symbol of healing, joins us together now. When we take steps to eliminate prejudice, we help heal our community and can become more faithful to the teachings of Jesus. *[Pull on the bandage till the person furthest away can feel the tug.]* Note that when one person is hurt, the whole community is affected.

[Unwrap one person's wrist and have them step outside the circle so the bandage falls limp.] When someone ignores the prejudice and is not part of the circle of healing, the community is fractured and incomplete. Listen now as I pray for an end to prejudice.

Lord, God of unity, Creator, Redeemer, and Spirit, you call us to love each person as our neighbor. Help us to put an end to prejudice, to be living examples of unity, and to be builders of your Kingdom where all are welcome. We pray in the name of Jesus Christ, who loved all people without boundaries or conditions. Amen.

Session Follow-Up

Family Connection

Direct the young people to ask their parents about the prejudicial attitudes they experienced when growing up. How did those prejudices affect them? Have the young people find out what their parents believe are the major prejudices affecting society and families today. Urge them to explore how their family can help heal those prejudices.

Daily Reading and Reflection

ScriptureWalk Bookmark

Distribute to the participants the bookmark for this session, found in appendix B. Point out that the bookmark has questions and scriptural passages on it. Invite them to deepen their understanding of the scriptural teaching on prejudice over the next several days by reading the passages and reflecting or journaling on the questions.

Scrambled Scripture Story

Copy this resource for use in step 1 of the Study It component. When you are ready to begin the activity, ask the participants for suggestions for each blank. You will need to tell them what the category is under each blank, but do not read the story aloud until all the blanks have been filled in.

A man was going down from _____ to
[geographic location]

_____ and fell into the hands of robbers, who stripped
[another geographic location]

him, beat him, and went away, leaving him half dead. Now by chance a

_____ was going down that road; and when she saw him,
[occupation]

she _____. So likewise a _____ passed by,
[verb, past tense]   [another occupation]

and when he came to the place and saw the beaten man, he

_____. But a _____, while traveling
[verb, paste tense]   [nationality]

came near him; and when she saw him, she was moved with

_____. She went to him and _____ his
[an emotion]   [verb, past tense]

wounds, having poured _____ and _____ on
[a liquid]   [another liquid]

them. Then she put him on her own _____, brought him
[animal]

to a _____, and took care of him. The next day she took
[name of a hotel]

out _____, gave it to the innkeeper, and said, "Take care of
[amount of money]

him; and when I _____, I will _____."
[verb]   [another verb]

Stress

Matthew 6:25–34

It is ironic that although we live in an age of convenience, people's stress levels seem greater than ever. Stress can distract us from what is truly important in life and diminish our quality of life by stealing our joy. Young people need help in avoiding stressful lives like those they see many older people living. In this passage from Matthew's Sermon on the Mount, Jesus counsels us to avoid needless anxiety and stress by remembering God's loving care for us.

 # Study It

Don't Worry, Trust in God (45–60 minutes)

Materials Needed

☐ newsprint and a marker (optional)
☐ masking tape (optional)
☐ Bibles, one for each person
☐ pens or pencils

Before the Session

☐ Write the words for the opening activity on newsprint (optional).
☐ If you plan to have a student proclaim the Scriptures in step 2, tell him or her ahead of time so that he or she can practice.
☐ Decide how you will present the commentary in step 4 (see p. 12 of the introduction for options).

Step 1

Opening Activity (10 minutes)

Tell the participants that you are about to read a list of things that cause stress in people's lives, and that they should raise one hand each time you name something that causes stress in their life and raise both hands each time you name something that causes a lot of stress. Explain that they can raise their hands as many times as they want. If you choose to, keep a record on a sheet of paper (or on the newsprint list of words, if you posted one) of the number of hands shown for each item. After you finish reading the list, ask if the group would like to add any words. Get a show of hands for each word added. If you kept track of the number of hands, announce which three stressors had the most hands up.

school	losing	homework
arguments	dating	college
parents	clothes	work
peer pressure	church	fear
grades	teachers	violence
money	loneliness	the future
sports	the car	

Step 2

Proclamation (5 minutes)

Invite the young people to think about their most stressful item from the list you read aloud as they listen to this Bible passage. Ask them to imagine that Jesus is speaking directly to them. Direct the young people to open their Bible to Matthew 6:25–34 so that they can follow along as the passage is proclaimed. When everyone is ready, proclaim Matthew 6:25–34, or if you have asked a student to do so, instruct him or her to begin.

Step 3   **Initial Reaction (10 minutes)**

Lead a brief discussion using the following questions. If your group is large, break it into small groups of five to eight people for this step. Have the group members refer to Matthew 6:25–34 in their Bible, as necessary.

- What word or phrase from the passage stood out as you listened to the reading?
- What do young people worry about?
- It is said that some people tend to live in the past, wishing they could change what has already happened. Some people live in the future, always worrying about what is to come. Some wise few live in the present, seeing and enjoying all that life is offering them right now. Of the three, where do you tend to live?

Step 4   **Commentary (5 minutes)**

After the discussion deliver the following commentary in the manner of your choice (see p. 12 of the introduction for options):

- The passage that we read is part of a long speech by Jesus in chapters 5 to 7 of Matthew, called the Sermon on the Mount. It is thought that the author of Matthew collected many of Jesus' teachings and sayings in this speech to present them in an organized and authoritative way. Some of the most familiar and important teachings of our faith are found in this speech, including the Lord's Prayer, the Beatitudes, the Golden Rule, and the words about turning the other cheek.

  Jesus' lesson on worry and anxiety, like many of the teachings from the Sermon on the Mount, uses images that were familiar to his audience. The lilies of the field spoken of in this passage were a kind of flower that bloomed for a short period of time and then were gathered up like dry grass or twigs, to get a fire started quickly. The birds he mentions were so common that most people took them for granted. Yet even these passing, seemingly insignificant bits of nature were cared for by God and were part of God's beautiful creation.

  Then to teach us about the uselessness of worrying, Jesus uses a kind of argument called "from the lesser to the greater." If God cares for such little things as birds and flowers, God surely cares much more for human beings! Wild animals don't worry about the future, and still they survive and have what they need. Isn't the same thing even more true for us? If God gave us the gift of life, doesn't it make sense that God would also provide what we need to sustain life?

  We must be careful not to interpret this passage to mean that Jesus is suggesting that people lead reckless lives with no thought for the future. Rather, he teaches that when planning for the future turns into anxiety, we are the losers. Stress, fear, and worry are the thieves that steal human joy. Jesus says in the Gospel of John, "I came that you might have life and have it to the full" (10:10). When we let worries cause us continual stress, we do not live fully. We miss God's gifts to us in the present moment, and we are only half alive.

In just a few sentences, Jesus reminds his listeners that it is the people who do not believe in God who strive for earthly security. Those who trust in God believe that God will care for them just as God cares for all creation. The stress caused by excessive worry is a symptom of a lack of faith. If a person doesn't believe in God's loving care for him or her or has no understanding of the constancy of God, that person becomes a victim of worry and is at its mercy. Jesus offers his listeners a solution: put God first, pay attention to the way God would have things, and then everything else will fall into place.

Step 5 ## Application (15-30 minutes)

Use the following questions to involve the participants in further discussion on how Matthew 6:25–34 applies to their life. You may wish to rephrase or add to these questions to tailor them to your group.

- Do you think people's lives were less stressful in Jesus' time? Why or why not?

- How does Jesus' teaching run contrary to the way people live in our culture?

- Do you think that certain advertisements, movies, news programs, and television shows encourage people's stress and anxiety? If so, can you give some examples?

- What happens to people physically, emotionally, and mentally when they get stressed out? What happens to their relationships with family members? with friends?

- What do you worry about?

- If there is a message in this passage for you, what is it?

- Jesus says we should "strive first" for the Kingdom. Why is it so hard to place our trust in God and not worry?

 # Live It

Climbing Back Up the Downward Spiral
(15–30 minutes)

This Live It activity uses the image of a spiral to symbolize how worry can drag us down toward stress and illness and, conversely, how focusing on God's goodness can bring us back up to peace and health.

Materials Needed

☐ copies of handout 8–A, "Stress Spinners," one for each person
☐ several pairs of scissors
☐ pens or pencils
☐ a tape or CD player, and a recording of reflective instrumental music (optional)
☐ yarn or string
☐ colored markers (optional)

Before the Session

☐ Before the session cut out one stress spinner from a copy of handout 8–A.

Step 1

When doing this component as an independent activity. If you are doing this component independent from the other session components, at the beginning of this step, you may want to proclaim Matthew 6:25–34 and share the commentary in step 4 of the Study It component.

Have everyone brainstorm as many things as they can that people experience stress over. If they have trouble getting started, try naming different groups of people—parents, teenagers, people who are dating, old people, children, working people, athletes, and so on—and asking, "What does this group worry about?" Record the stressors the group comes up with on the back of the precut stress spinner.

Now have a student volunteer hold the top of the stress spinner you have created. Present the points below in your own words, following the directions in brackets as you do so:
• Jesus warns his followers that worry has no purpose. It is a waste of time and energy. When we let worry and stress take hold of us, they drag us down. *[Grab the bottom of the stress spinner and pull down, stretching it out.]*
• Worry is worse than useless; it hurts us. Needless worry takes the joy out of life. Getting into the habit of worrying can lead to broken relationships, an inability to make decisions, a loss of the gifts and skills we have, fear, loneliness, and depression. *[Pull down until the stress spinner tears and breaks.]*

- The stress that needless worry causes is like a weight on our soul. It can pull us away from God. The ultimate result of uncontrolled stress is the loss of our physical, emotional, and spiritual health—a diminishment of God's precious gift of life. *[Keep pulling on the stress spinner, tearing off pieces until nothing is left.]*

Step 2

Pass out to each person a copy of handout 8–A, "Stress Spinners," a pen or pencil, and a pair of scissors. Suggest that one way to counter-act stress is to take time to remember God's goodness and to remind ourselves of God's care for us by counting our blessings. Ask the young people to take a few minutes alone to write on the back of their hand-out all the people, relationships, gifts, skills, and experiences for which they would like to thank God. While they are working, if you wish, play a recording of reflective instrumental music.

When everyone is done writing, tell them to cut out their stress spinner along the dotted line. Pass out yarn or string and tell them to tie a piece of it to the end of their spinner for hanging. If you have time, distribute colored markers and invite the young people to deco-rate their spinner. When everyone is finished, invite each person to share with the group a few of the things she or he is thankful for. Sug-gest that they take their spinner home and hang it as a reminder to let go of their worries and trust in God's care. Or you can hang the spin-ners in your youth room or meeting space.

Alternative Approach

"Christ's Little Instruction Book"

Prepare for this activity by cutting 8½-by-11-inch sheets of paper into 4¼-by-5½ inch quarters. Cut enough sheets of paper so that each participant has ten to fifteen of these quarter sheets.

When everyone is ready, explain that they will be using the entire Sermon on the Mount (Matthew, chapters 5–7) as a resource to each create a "Christ's Little Instruction Book." Give each participant ten to fifteen of the quarter sheets you prepared, along with pens and markers for writing and decorating.

Direct the participants to read through the Sermon on the Mount and to note the sections or phrases that stand out for them. Tell them to paraphrase, that is, put into their own words, at least eight sections or phrases, writing one on each sheet of paper. For example, they might rewrite Matthew 6:1–7, a passage on almsgiving and prayer, as "Don't make a show of good deeds and prayer. These things should come from your heart."

Encourage them to decorate their pages and a cover page. When everyone is done, staple each person's pages together along the left margin, creating a booklet.

Suggest to the young people that they keep their booklet as a keepsake or give it to a younger person, a friend, or a family member.

 # Pray It

Let God Fill You! (15 minutes)

Materials Needed

☐ a candle and matches
☐ a Bible
☐ a clear glass half filled with water
☐ a pitcher full of water
☐ a copy of the prayer script

Before the Session

☐ Place the following items in the prayer area: a candle, an open Bible, a clear glass half filled with water, and a pitcher full of water.
☐ Give a volunteer reader a copy of the prayer script to look over.

Prayer Directions

When you are ready, dim the lights, light the candle, and call the group to prayer.

Leader. Creator God, you made the birds of the air and the flowers of the field. You created each of us as well. You know all our needs and all our worries. Hear us now as we come to you in prayer. *[Pause.]*

Reader. [Slowly] The half-empty glass is really a trick, an optical illusion. . . . Its emptiness is not a fact; it is only a misperception, an observation made by a misunderstanding watcher. . . . In fact, the empty half of the glass is really full. It might be full of worry: Will I have enough? Where and when and how will I get more? What if somebody sees me half empty like this and doesn't like me?

The empty half of the glass is really full. . . . It might be full of hope, peace, waiting to be filled to overflowing with God's loving presence.

[Reader fills the glass to the top with water.]

Leader. God fills each of us like this . . . with rich gifts, with friendship, with everything that we need. Lord, help us to focus not on our own worries and needs but on you and your Kingdom. Help us to remember your goodness and to trust that you will provide all the things we truly need. Let us take a few moments to thank God, either silently or aloud, for the gifts God has given us.

[Take time for shared, spontaneous prayer.]

Leader. Let us close our prayer by saying together the prayer of trust in God that Jesus taught his disciples, the Lord's Prayer.

Session Follow-Up

Family Connection

Invite the participants to take home an extra copy of handout 8–A, "Stress Spinners." Either give them the following directions verbally or make copies to send home with them:

• Reflect with your family members on causes of stress or worry in their life. Then reflect together on all the blessings in your family's life and write them on the spinner. Cut the spinner out and hang it in a place where everyone in the family will pass by it and be reminded of all the good things in their life. Explain to your family that remembering God's goodness to them in the past can help build trust in God for the future.

Daily Reading and Reflection

ScriptureWalk Bookmark

Distribute to the participants the bookmark for this session, found in appendix B. Point out that the bookmark has questions and scriptural passages on it. Invite the young people to deepen their understanding of the scriptural teaching on stress and peace over the next several days by reading the passages and reflecting or journaling on the questions.

Stress Spinners

Before cutting out the spiral, write on the back of it all the people, relationships, gifts, skills, and experiences for which you would like to thank God. Then cut along the dotted line to create your stress spinner. Tie a piece of yarn or string to the narrow end of the spiral so that you can hang it.

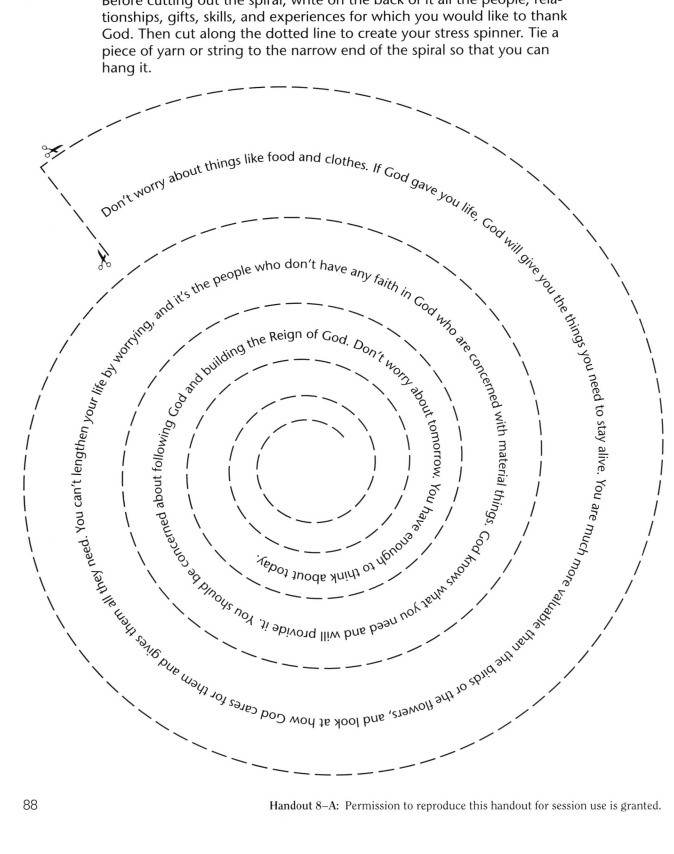

Don't worry about things like food and clothes. If God gave you life, God will give you the things you need to stay alive. You are much more valuable than the birds or the flowers, and look at how God cares for them and gives them all they need. You can't lengthen your life by worrying, and it's the people who don't have any faith in God who are concerned with material things. God knows what you need and will provide it. You should be concerned about following God and building the Reign of God. Don't worry about tomorrow. You have enough to think about today.

Handout 8–A: Permission to reproduce this handout for session use is granted.

What the Scriptures Say . . . and Don't Say: Reading the Bible in Context

by Margaret Nutting Ralph

Have you ever heard two people who totally disagree with each other use Scripture to "prove" that God is on their side? Instead of letting the Scriptures form their thinking, they use a quote from the Scriptures, often taken out of context, to support their own opinions.

We've probably all done this to some extent. Even expert theologians use Scripture quotes to show that their teaching is rooted in the Bible. But a proper understanding of biblical revelation will challenge us to examine our approach to the Scriptures and overcome any tendency to quote the Bible out of context.

Instead of asking, "Do these words support what I already think?" we need to ask, "What is this passage trying to teach me?" When we recognize what the inspired biblical authors intended to teach, we are opening our minds and hearts to the revelation of the Scriptures.

The revealed Scriptures do not necessarily hold the same meaning we may want to attach to the words. The inspired biblical authors intended to say and teach certain truths, and we need to root our understanding of the Scriptures first and foremost in the intent of the author.

But how do we determine the intentions of an author who lived thousands of years ago in a totally different cultural setting? The church teaches us that in order to understand the revelation the Bible contains, we must learn first and foremost to read passages in the context in which they appear.

What are you reading? One way to safeguard against misunderstanding the intent of an author is to determine the kind of writing the author has chosen to use. Any piece of writing has a particular literary form: poetry, prose, fiction, essay, letter, historical account, and so on. This is as true of the biblical books as of any piece of contemporary writing.

If we misunderstand an author's literary form, we will misunderstand what the author intends to say. In order to understand what we are reading, then, we have to make allowances for the form and change our expectations accordingly.

We do this any time we read a newspaper, for example. As we turn the pages of a newspaper, we encounter a variety of literary forms—news, features, editorials, and so on—and we adjust our idea of what we can expect from the writing for each form.

For instance, after I read a news story, I expect to have the answer to the question What happened? I expect the author of a news story to be objective and evenhanded, to inform me of the facts. If the story is about something controversial, I expect the writer to cover all sides fairly.

When I get to the editorial page, I change my expectations. Now I know that the author is allowed to be persuasive rather than objective. I may find facts that support the author's point of view but nothing that contradicts that point of view.

So if I read an editorial with the same frame of mind with which I read a front-page news story, thinking that the author has responded to the question What happened?, I will be misinformed after I finish my reading. It is not the author's fault that I am misinformed. It is my own.

How the inspired author tells the tale. Now lets look at how literary form functions in the Bible. One of the inspired biblical authors—the author of the Book of Job—has written in the form of a debate. This literary form demands that you be as persuasive as possible on both sides of an issue. If you write persuasively on the side you agree with and poorly on the side you disagree with, you have not written a good debate.

The author of the Book of Job lived at a time when people believed that all suffering was punishment for sin. He wrote a debate to argue against this belief. The author places his debate in the context of a pre-existing legend that establishes at the outset the fact that Job is innocent. So why is he suffering?

The author portrays Job's friends arguing with Job over the cause of his suffering. All the friends think that Job must have sinned or he wouldn't be suffering. They do not know, as does the audience, that Job's sinfulness is not the source of his suffering. The friends are wrong.

Now, if you did not know that the Book of Job is a debate, in which some of the characters argue persuasively for the point of view with which the author disagrees, you might read an isolated passage and conclude that the book teaches the opposite of what the author intended to teach. You might think that the friends are teaching a valid message about suffering.

If we look at the book as a whole, we discover that the author places the truth he is teaching not on the lips of Job's friends but on the lips of God. God appears at the end of the debate and responds to the friends' arguments. Obviously, the author agrees with what God has to say. God contradicts the belief that all suffering is punishment for sin.

Because this book is in the canon, we know that it teaches revealed truth. We can only discover this revealed truth, however, if we look at the literary form of the book.

We need to remember, too, that the Bible is actually a "library" of many different books. To say that Job is a debate is not to say that the Bible as a whole is a debate or that a Gospel is a debate or that the Book of Revelation is a debate. The answer to the question What literary form am I reading? will vary from book to book. Often the introduction to each book in a good study Bible will give you the relevant literary form.

Culture in context. We have seen how easy it is to "misquote" the Bible by taking passages out of the context of their literary form. A second context we need to consider is the culture and the beliefs in place when the book was written. The inspired author and the original audience shared knowledge, presumptions, expressions, and concerns that may not be part of our awareness, but may nevertheless influence the meaning of the book or passage.

The inspired author may have applied the revealed message contained in a particular book to a shared cultural setting in order to make the message clearer. People sometimes mistake such applications for the heart of the revealed message. Thus they put the full authority of the Scriptures behind passages that reflect beliefs of the time rather than the unchanging truth the author intended to teach.

In expressing the revealed truth, a biblical author may show cultural biases and presumptions that later generations know are inaccurate. This kind of misunderstanding resulted in Galileo's excommunication. We know, as biblical authors did not, that the earth is not the center of the universe or even our solar system. We also know that the Bible does not claim to teach astronomy. Rather, the Bible addresses questions about the relationship between God and God's people, about what we should be doing to build up God's Kingdom rather than to tear it down.

A biblical author may also apply an eternal truth to a setting that is important to the original audience but not to us. For example, one of Paul's key insights is that the way we treat every other person is the way we treat the risen Christ. He applies this insight to the social order of his own day, an order that included slavery. We misuse the Scriptures if we say this application shows that *God's* social order includes slavery. While Paul's core message is eternally true revelation, the application was relevant only in its own cultural context.

Revelation is ongoing. A third context we must be aware of is the place the inspired author's insights have in the process of revelation. The Bible is not a book of bottom-line answers like a catechism.

The Bible is a "library of books" written over a two-thousand-year period. It reflects the process by which the inspired authors came to greater knowledge of God's revealed truth. People who do not realize or do not believe that the Bible reflects this progression take an early insight as the whole truth.

For example, people may make this mistake when arguing over the death penalty. Some people who support the death penalty try to put God's authority behind their opinion by quoting Scripture: An eye for an eye, a tooth for a tooth, a life for a life.

It is true that the Scriptures teach this (see Ex. 21:23–24). However, the teaching dates to the time of Exodus, about 1250 B.C.E. At the time, this teaching was an ethical step forward. It taught people not to seek escalating revenge: If you harm me, I can't do worse to you than you originally did to me.

Jesus later challenged people to grow beyond this teaching. He said, "You have heard that it was said, 'an eye for an eye and a tooth for a tooth. . . .' But I say to you, Love your enemies and pray for those who persecute you" (Matthew 5:38–44). Jesus did not say that the law was wrong, only that it did not go far enough. Jesus is the fulfillment of the law.

We are misusing the Scriptures if we quote Exodus to support the death penalty and fail to quote the words of Jesus in the Gospels. When we use a passage from the Scriptures to support our side of an argument, we must ask ourselves if the passage reflects the fullness of truth or whether it is a partial truth, perhaps an early insight.

Context, context, context. It is distressing to hear Christians abuse the Bible by quoting it in favor of unchristian positions. It is doubly distressing to realize that we ourselves might be guilty of this.

One way to avoid this mistake is to remember always to consider the context. Determine the place of a passage in its larger context. Ask yourself what literary form the author is using. Explore the beliefs and presumptions the author may share with the original audience. Learn something about the time when the book was written. Know how the author's insights fit into the process of revelation.

If we do this, we will avoid many a harmful error. We will be less likely to abuse the Scriptures and more likely to hear the revelation of God's love that the biblical authors intend us to hear.

Finally, invite the Holy Spirit to open up your mind and heart as you listen to the word. Discerning God's will in your life will leave you with Christ's own peace in your heart.

Margaret Nutting Ralph is secretary for educational ministries for the Diocese of Lexington, Kentucky, and director of the master's degree programs for Roman Catholics at Lexington Theological Seminary. She has taught the Scriptures to high school students, college students, and adult education groups for twenty years. She is the author of the book and video *And God Said What?* and the Discovering the Living Word series (all from Paulist Press).

ScriptureWalk Bookmarks

Forgiveness

Day 1: Psalm 51*
- Psalm 51 is a very well known psalm of lament prayed by King David. Which verses speak most clearly to you at this time in your life?
- Spend some time telling God where you need forgiveness in order to be healed of sin and guilt.

Day 2: Matthew 18:21–35*
- Is there someone you have stopped short of going the distance (seventy times seven times) for in your willingness to forgive her or him? Why?
- If God searched your heart right now, what would God see as the obstacles that are blocking you from forgiving this person?

Day 3: Genesis 45:1–15*
- Joseph's willingness to forgive his brothers' evil acts allowed God to work through him to accomplish something good. Recall a time when giving or receiving forgiveness allowed God to work through you.

Day 4: John 8:1–11
- Have you ever felt that you have done something that is beyond the forgiveness of Christ? If so, who can you talk to about it?
- What are the "stones of judgement"—your prejudices and unforgiving attitudes—that you carry?

Day 5: 1 John 2:7–11*
- Is there anything that is causing darkness in your life right now?
- What actions can you take this week in order to return to the light of God?

*The readings marked by an asterisk have companion articles in *The Catholic Youth Bible.*

Family

Day 1: Sirach 3:1–16*
- In raising you, what are some of the things that your parents have done that you would someday like to do for your children?
- Does any part of this passage make you angry, sad, or uncomfortable? Write a letter to God about your feelings.

Day 2: Ephesians 5:21— 6:4*
- What does this passage teach you about the relationships between parents and children?
- This passage implies that believing in Christ makes a difference in the way family members relate to one another. How does Christian faith make a difference in a family's life together?

Day 3: Colossians 3:18*
- How would you describe your relationship with your parents? When is it most difficult to obey them?
- Name some of the characteristics of the love shared in your family (for example, gentle or courageous). How have these characteristics shaped your understanding of God?

Day 4: Matthew 7:12
- Think of something that causes conflict or tension in your family. How would this be different if you applied the Golden Rule?

Day 5: Joshua 24:14–15*
- What are the ways that your family lives out its religious commitment?
- Are there other things you wish your family would do in practicing your faith together?

*The readings marked by an asterisk have companion articles in *The Catholic Youth Bible.*

Anger

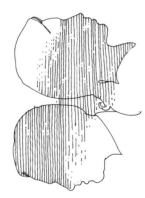

Day 1: Psalm 43*
- Which verse of this psalm best describes how you feel when you are angry?
- Reread the psalm and listen for the whispers of hope contained within its words. What has ruled your emotions this week—anger or hope?

Day 2: Matthew 5:21–26
- These are strong words by Jesus. How do they make you feel?
- Is God calling you to reconcile with someone this week? What steps do you need to take to do so?

Day 3: John 2:13–17*
- What injustices and public sins should cause Christians today to experience righteous anger like Jesus did in this passage?
- What particular values is God calling you to uphold and defend at this time in your life?

Day 4: Proverbs 22:24–25*
- How do your friends and members of your family express anger? Have they been positive models or negative models for you?
- Is God calling you to change how you express your anger? In what way?

Day 5: James 1:19–25
- Be honest: How well do your actions reflect Jesus' values and teachings?
- What words—that is, what beliefs and behaviors— is God trying to plant in you?

*The readings marked by an asterisk have companion articles in *The Catholic Youth Bible.*

Love

Day 1: Song of Solomon 8:6–7
- How do you know about lasting love? Who has modeled for you what a steadfast love is all about?
- God's love for you is infinitely deeper than the deepest love you may have experienced from another person. Spend some time reflecting on this in prayer.

Day 2: Matthew 5:43–48*
- What challenges you about this definition of love?
- Who is God leading you to love like this? It might be someone very close to you.

Day 3: Romans 8:31–39*
- What in your life tends to separate you from the love of God? from the love of your family and friends?
- Ask God to strengthen all your relationships and for the faith to believe in the power of God's love.

Day 4: 1 John 3:16–18*
- When was the last time you showed this type of compassionate love to another? Why did you?
- What is God asking you to do this week in order that God's love can shine forth from you?

Day 5: Mark 12:28–31
- How would you rate yourself, on a scale of 1 to 10, in living out the law of love this week?
- What are some of your other "loves"—the selfish attitudes or behaviors you hang on to—that keep you from fully embracing this greatest commandment?

*The readings marked by an asterisk have companion articles in *The Catholic Youth Bible*.

Hope

Day 1: Psalm 14*
- What situations are crushing your hope at this time?
- Make up your own song or prayer of distress to God. Let God be part of your trying times.

Day 2: Matthew 27:45–54*
- Can you see the hope in this story of Jesus' death? The cross is both a sign of death and the beginning of new life. How can this understanding help you through the dark and difficult times of life?
- Spend some time reflecting on the cross as a sign of hope. Ask God to be with you through whatever hopelessness you experience this week.

Day 3: Romans 8:18–28*
- How difficult is it for you to place your hope and trust in a God you cannot see, in a future that isn't clear?
- In the stillness of prayer, allow the Holy Spirit to speak to God on your behalf.

Day 4: 2 Corinthians 4:7–18*
- What are the ways in which you are feeling afflicted, discouraged, or weighed down right now?
- If Jesus defeated sin and death, then what can he do with your burdens if you allow him the chance?

Day 5: Revelation 21:1–4 and 22:20–21
- What experience of hope do you get when you read these last words of the Scriptures?
- How do your life and actions offer hope to others?

*The readings marked by an asterisk have companion articles in *The Catholic Youth Bible*.

Friendship

Day 1: Ruth 1:1–17
- Have you had friends you were so close to that you could not imagine being separated?
- What can you learn from your friendships about God's love for you?

Day 2: 1 Samuel, chapter 20*
- What were the characteristics of David and Jonathan's friendship?
- What lesson or meaning is in this story for you?

Day 3: John 15:12–17
- Reflect on the ways that you and your friends lay down your lives for one another.
- What might God be saying to you through this passage?

Day 4: Acts 11:19–26*
- Barnabas brought the gift of encouragement to his friends. What gifts do you bring to your friendships?
- Think of someone you know who is going through a hard time. What can you do to encourage that person?

Day 5: Genesis 28:10–22*
- In this story, Jacob and God promise devotion to each other. What kind of devotion do you feel God has to you? Is it mutual?
- What steps might you take to deepen your friendship with God?

*The readings marked by an asterisk have companion articles in *The Catholic Youth Bible*.

Stress

Day 1: Psalm 22*
- Have you ever felt abandoned, under attack, or alone like the person in this psalm?
- Use the second part of this passage (verses 19–31) as a prayer of praise and thanksgiving.

Day 2: Philippians 4:4–9*
- How can you rejoice when times are hard?
- What worries is God calling you from?

Day 3: Psalm 27
- Reflect on a time when your belief and confidence in God were as strong as those of the person in this psalm. How would a stronger faith help you live a less stressful life?

Day 4: Isaiah 11:1–9*
- Imagine yourself living in the Kingdom described here. How might God be calling you to live more peacefully? How would your life be different if you did?

Day 5: Psalm 91*
- How does God protect you? How can God be a refuge for you?
- What kinds of fears keep you from trusting in God?

*The readings marked by an asterisk have companion articles in *The Catholic Youth Bible*.

Prejudice

Day 1: Romans 14:1–12*
- Reflect on a time when you felt someone was biased against you because of your beliefs.
- When have you judged someone else negatively because of their beliefs? What might God be saying to you through this passage?

Day 2: Acts 11:1–18*
- What groups seem to be excluded from full participation in church and society today?
- What do Christians need to do to be more inclusive in their outreach to others?

Day 3: Ruth 2:1–16*
- Boaz easily could have overlooked Ruth as just another insignificant poor person. Why do you think he did not do so?
- Who are the people in your school or community who are easily overlooked? What might you do to notice them?

Day 4: Luke 9:46–48
- Jesus reminds us that the world's view of greatness is not God's view. Among the people you know, who would Jesus rank as great in God's eyes?
- How might Jesus be calling you to focus less on the world's values and more on God's values?

Day 5: Luke 10:25–37*
- Jesus' listeners were shocked to hear that a Samaritan was the hero. Who in today's society would you be shocked to see portrayed as a hero?
- What could you do to recognize and help eliminate prejudice in your community?

*The readings marked by an asterisk have companion articles in *The Catholic Youth Bible*.